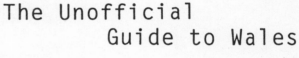

The Unofficial
        Guide to Wales

First impression: February 1994
© Y Lolfa Cyf., 1994

Text by:
COLIN PALFREY
ARWEL ROBERTS

Cartoons and cover picture by:
ELWYN IOAN

Photographs by:
KEITH MORRIS
ALED JENKINS

ISBN: 0 86243 309 6

Printed and published in Wales
by Y Lolfa Cyf., Talybont, Ceredigion SY24 5HE;
tel. (0970) 832 304, *fax* 832 782.

The Unofficial Guide to Wales

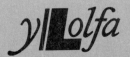

Introduction

Most people who come to Wales are struck by the sheer unspoilt beauty of the countryside. Even in the industrialised (well, formerly anyway) valleys of South Wales the rural atmosphere is all around. From Tredegar to Tonypandy, from Pontlottyn to Porth, you can still enjoy being surrounded by sheep and mountain ponies—even in your bathroom if you're lucky enough to have one. But wherever you stay in Wales the mountains are never far away, beckoning. Only a pony-trek away from Merthyr, for example, the Brecon Beacons beckon. But beware—the area can be dangerous, for more than one experienced climber has been found among the mist-swirled ledges, in a horizontal position, his packed lunch only half-eaten.

In North Wales as in most of the attractive, get-away-from-it-all areas, local Welsh-speaking groups offer guided tours of holiday homes. If

you're tempted to rent one of these delightful retreats try to avoid booking during the off-peak (October-April) as forest fires and spontaneous combustion have been known to affect these properties from time to time.

When you think of Wales you probably think of singing. Everyone in Wales can sing—and everybody does on all occasions. While singing at rugby matches, funerals and sheep-shearing contests is commonplace, how many visitors to Wales realise that Council business is also conducted in song? This is an honourable tradition that goes back far beyond the era of Aneurin Bevan or even Ivor Novello. The Welsh are famed for the sing-song quality of their speech and their feeling for language, but to sit in a District or County Council meeting—as unfortunately few local people choose to do—is a veritable feast of music and drama, from the Grand Opera of Annual General Meeting to the operettas of planning and environmental health sub-committees. Differing councils have different styles, as you might expect. One large County Council, for example, usually intones the

minutes in plainsong rather rapidly with staccato responses from the majority chorus. This is accompanied by mournful dirge-like undertones from the minority wind section or by high-pitched pizzicatos from individual members.

In some valley councils, on the other hand, there have been times when the musical renditions of melody and counterpoint have reached truly Wagnerian proportion, much to the surprise and delight of the small but loyal audiences attracted to these regular extravaganzas. Indeed, at one time the audience was frequently inspired to take part, providing a spontaneous but often cacophonous choral backing. This kind of audience participation has, however, tended to lapse recently as the Council can no longer afford to provide musical scores for everyone in the auditorium. In fact, many of those taking part in the official majority chorus are no longer provided with music sheets. They have learned their parts off by heart and only occasionally do they require a cue from the leading players to come in. They have also mastered the art of sleeping with their eyes open, as has the conductor of the proceedings—known as the Chairman—when the minor characters are singing off-key.

Admission to these performances is free but not yet obligatory. There are sometimes matinée or late-night sessions but most of them end in good time for the leading players to go off and rehearse for the next show. Advance bookings can be made but visitors should check with the Clerk to make sure that the content of any particular meeting is suitable for children and old-age pensioners.

The National Eisteddfod

This festival of the arts attracts many thousands of visitors every year. It is the one major event in which everything is conducted through the medium of the Welsh language, except for the sculptures which tend to be mute and sometimes English. One of the main competitions is open to all visitors and takes place in the big tent or pavilion. This is the (in translation) Audience Endurance Medal and is awarded to the member of the public who can remain in his/her seat (visits to the *tŷ bach* permitted) through a minimum of ten renderings of the same folk song, five clog dances, twenty-four choral recitations and at least thirty-five individual adjudications. The record for this stamina-sapping event is held by a farmer from Ceredigion whose hobby is listed in the Eisteddfod's 'Who's Who' as counting three-legged sheep. The climax of the week is the Chairing of the Bard. In the past this prize has been withheld because the actual chair was not considered to be of a satisfactory standard.

(One—like the farmer's sheep—had only three legs!).

8

Another interesting event in the annual Urdd Eisteddfod is the children's choral singing. Here you can see earnest teachers coaxing the maximum performance out of well-drilled pupils all singing in tune and bending their heads forward at the statutory dip of fifteen degrees. The choir which can go the longest time without laughing at their conductor's facial contortions is declared the winner. There is a complex scale of points that are subtracted from the maximum of twenty. For example, two points are taken off for a titter, five for a fairly obvious and outright giggle, ten for a guffaw and if any chorister is seen rolling on the floor in uncontrollable laughter the whole choir is automatically disqualified.

Nowadays the highly complicated construction of traditional Welsh verse forms on which the major prizes are based are worked out on computers, so in theory anyone can enter. Indeed, the last two winners of the formal verse competitions have been a retired wine waiter from Blaenau Ffestiniog and 'A Welsh speaking budgie from Rhyl'—the words in quotes being a translation of the opening line of the winning epic poem produced on microcomputer by the feathered bard.

The Gorsedd at a secret location.

But much of the attraction of the National Eisteddfod is the social life that takes place on the *maes* (field) outside the main pavilion. Here there are side-stalls galore where you can drop in for a quick protest and demo and totally alcohol-free caterers' tents where, for a few pounds, you can enjoy the traditional Welsh fare of half a ham sandwich and a plastic cup of Espresso tea.

Perhaps the most emotional part of the whole festival is the day when visitors from overseas are given a tumultuous *croeso* (welcome). This moment belongs to all those Welsh exiles who decided long ago to settle and make a few relatively tax-free dollars. In one mass migration they return in August to wherever the Eisteddfod is being held. There is a special tent set aside for them staffed by medical personnel. So if you should notice a long line of senior citizens, some of them in funny hats and most of them sporting cameras, you will probably be witnessing the Inoculation Ceremony. In a secret location somewhere in the North a pure Welsh culture has been preserved by members of the *Gorsedd* (see below). A minute quantity of this culture is injected into the visitors from other lands in order to top up their Welshness for another twelve months. A precise dose of the culture must be administered—too little, and they may never return; too much, and they may be tempted to sell up and buy Anglesey.

The Eisteddfod is also a venue for the Welsh alternative to a week-long 18-30 holiday-cum-beer festival, although no ID cards are needed to tell that most of the revellers are still in the throes of pubescent rebellion. This unwashed and uninhibited species overcomes the no-alcohol rule simply by avoiding the Eisteddfod field and spending the whole week wreaking havoc in public houses and recreating a not-so-peaceful Woodstock scenario in the no adult zone tent site.

The Gorsedd on a bus.

Flora and fauna

For the nature lover there can be few more exciting places to spend a holiday than Wales. Here, in a small land, are numerous varieties of animal life not seen anywhere else in the world—species left undiscovered by Darwin, genetic throwbacks to a more primeval era in our history.

There are sanctuaries in Wales devoted to the preservation and propagation of rare creatures. Here you may see the Cardiff pigeon that has over the years adapted to life in the city. At outdoor cafés you will see a family of these intelligent birds sitting around a table. If you're lucky they may toss you a few crumbs of a leftover sandwich; if you're unlucky you may come away with white shoulders. These fascinating birds have become the obsession of groups of grown men who meet in secret in the twilight zone of the major Welsh towns. Among the gay bars amd masonic halls you might notice a workmen's club or a disused church hall where within meets a circle of pigeon-fanciers. This pastime has an odd history, for the word 'fancy' appears now to have completely altered its meaning over the years. Now these ardent enemies of the humble pigeon go to great lengths to capture the brids, take them in trucks and cars to remote spots and let them go. Unfortunately, most of the birds fly back to their luckless captors only to have the same bizarre treatment inflicted on them week after week.

Other animals form the centrepiece of Welsh sports and shows. One of these is a lurcher—a cross between a border collie and a rug. This dog, with its ally the Welsh terrier, forms a deadly duo that has been known to flush from their holes rabbits, badgers, foxes and the occasional miner.

The Welsh corgi, so beloved by the Royal Family, is an aggressive little dog that bites the legs of cattle. They are known as the Welsh wing forwards of the animal kingdom. And what could be more typically Welsh than the sound of the shepherd whistling to his dog to round up the sheep and bring them home?

Perhaps the sound of his wife shouting to his dog to bring him home 'cause his dinner's ready. Among the sheep of Wales one breed stands out—the South Wales valley sheep, known officially as 'dafad acrobaticus'. Most farms of any size in South Wales have a gymnasium attached where, from an early age, the sheep are trained in the art of commando-style manœuvres. In order to eke out their meagre EC subsidies, the farmers in this part of Wales have to make sure their sheep gain access to every blade of grass available—from churchyards to back gardens. Walls, cattle grids and fences are no barrier to these engaging creatures. If they can't get over them they usually eat their way through them. Indeed, scientific tests have discovered in the intestines of dead valley sheep a whole range of objects such as leaves, wire wool, underpants and the complete works of R.S.Thomas (paperback edition).

Animals also play a central part in Welsh legend—is there really a monster in Bala Lake (*Llyn Tegid*)? Did dragons ever roam the mountains of Wales? Is it true that the ratio of

dogs per council house is 3.5 to 1?

But for the true symbols of Wales we turn to the humble leek and daffodil, which taste roughly the same. While there are few competitions to grow the biggest daffodil, local horticultural shows feature gigantic leeks, some as thick as a goalpost and tasting roughly the same. While these are easily recognisable, the lonely whinberry growing wild on moor and mountain can sometimes be mistaken for other less succulent offerings. Many a tourist, having spent ten hours half way up a Welsh mountain picking whinberries or bilberries has gone back to his self-catering chalet only to squander a vintage Burgundy on a pie whose main ingredient turned out to be sheep droppings.

Sport and recreation

There are two major sports in Wales: one is rugby, the other is pushing old cars off the tops of mountains. Both sports flourish in the valleys of South Wales and both share the same elements of danger, excitement and financial profit. If you're travelling to Wales then bring your old banger. Surely there can be no more exhilarating family fun than looking out over a Welsh valley and getting the wife and kids to help you push the car over the top. Then, after your holiday is over, claiming insurance money for your stolen vehicle. As the locals will tell you, there is an art in trying to get your car to end up in an interesting position—upside down, standing on its back wheels or perched on the TV aerial of some terraced house. One or two local authorities, far from clearing away these scrapped vehicles, have approached the Welsh Office to declare the sites areas of outstanding natural beauty ever since one motor graveyard was entered successfully for a sculpture competition at the National Eisteddfod (see text).

The National Stadium in Cardiff is the home of Welsh rugby. In Wales, rugby is said to be more of a religion than a sport—this is because in recent years the number of believers has declined. The game is highly competitive and virile. There are fifteen players in each team. Nowadays in Wales the game follows a very strict pattern. Six players stand absolutely still while another eight go into a huddle with their arms round each other. Occasionally the ball is thrown amongst them by another player. No tickling or horseplay is permitted in these huddles (scrums). The object of these set pieces is to hide the ball until the back seven players become restless and move. Once or twice the ball is actually passed to the backs to tempt them to run. Any player who does so is penalised by being sent off the field forthwith and being forced to watch the entire video of the 1983 Welsh Rugby Cup Final.

For those visitors to Wales who prefer to take part rather than just watch there are countless opportunities in sporting Wales. Try water-skiing on the moat around Caerphilly Castle;

you're sure to draw an appreciative crowd. Or why not book in for hang-gliding lessons in Cardiff. Jump off the top of the Pearl building and let the warm air currents blowing from the capital city's numerous Indian restaurants waft you where you will. Don't worry if you are carried further than you intended. Each hang-gliding participant is ringed by volunteers from the cardiff Pigeon Fanciers Club (see text). Wherever you may land, the hired equipment can be returned to the Cardiff City Council in the stamped addressed twelve foot square box that each hang-glider carries on his back.

In the North, for the really adventurous there is the challenge of Welsh rock-climbing. Giant sticks of rock bearing the message 'Llandudno lives' are thrust deep into the sand. Standing on the top of the rock on a clear day you can see the tip of 'Little England beyond Wales'. This is called 'Cardiff'.

Entertainment

From casinos to clog-dancing, telly to twmpath, Wales has it all. Choirs, harpists, folk-singers are ready to entertain you at the drop of a Welsh hat. Miners still go home two by two after a twelve hour shift singing in perfect harmony. Music and arts centres are springing up in all corners of Wales and these cater for all tastes—from chamber music and poetry readings to lectures on wool dyeing and exhibitions of contemporary toothpicks.

At the more avant-garde centres in the major towns and cities you can listen to a free lunchtime recital of early Bolivian love songs played on authentic flower pots or watch forgotten masterpieces of the cinema such as the Swedish 'Tribute to Spring', a three hour epic which portrays a marigold growing in slow motion. The *Cymanfa Ganu* is a vibrant event in the chapel calendar. No such gala of singing is complete without *Hwyl*—he is the conductor who will tell you when to stand up and sit down, when to sing loud or soft or when to whip round with the collection box. Everyone in the village attends the *Cymanfa;* if you don't they might be singing about you.

Eating and drinking

Mention Wales and you immediately think of laver-bread and cockles. Many visitors to Wales shy away from laver-bread because it looks rather like the third layer on a compost heap. At one time laver-bread was thought to have been processed from seaweed; nowadays it is more widely known that this typically Welsh fare is made from washing-up cloths impregnated with Guinness. Buy it from the local market where the friendly stall-holders will tell you what to do with it. If you're used to eating moss and sand with your bacon then laver-bread is for you.

Chitterlings are another traditional Welsh delicacy and are eaten ungarnished. In former days a necklace of chitterlings was said to keep diseases away, as well as most other people. *Cawl cennin* (leek soup) and lamb cooked in honey feature in the Welsh banquets now so popular throughout Wales. For those with less adventurous palates why not try the Welsh Wimpy—compressed chitterlings and laver-bread served up in a bap. Penclawdd cockles are another renowned Welsh dish. Some of these shell fish are so large that after you've eaten the inside you can use the shell as a boat to go fishing in—to catch more cockles.

Wales now boasts at least two native ales, and a distillery. While these drinks enjoy widespread popularity, the local wines have a distinctive bouquet and taste that must be acquired. Since there are now few vineyards in Wales, peas are used instead. There is not a more traditionally Welsh sight than a bevy of *y werin* up to their ankles in peas, treading the pods to make the instant vintage wine. Many a Welsh maiden aunt who would never dream of entering a pub will be happy enough to regale you, the visitors, with her home-made wine. After an hour or so you won't want to leave. After a few more hours you won't be able to! You may also like to enter the local beer-swilling competitions. These are usually held in rugby clubs where, for a nominal fee, you can be signed in by a member. The regulars welcome a sporting challenge but make sure that if you do enter as a competitor you don't actually win— especially if you're English.

Buildings

Of course, you cannot come to know Wales without visiting some of its historic monuments. Most impressive of these are the castles, from the colossal splendour of Caernarfon castle to the tiny folly of Castell Coch near Cardiff, or the extravaganza of Portmeirion inspired by a dream after the architect—William Clough Ellis—had been dining on smoked mackerel, pâté de foie gras and a tin of curried beans.

There are some outstanding religious buildings in Wales too. Carved into the rock at San Gofan in *Sir Benfro* (Pembrokeshire, now part of Dyfed) is probably the smallest chapel in Wales. In earlier times smugglers and puffins formed the major part of the congregation. Today it remains a sanctuary for the more hardy courting couples. St. David's Cathedral, Llandaf Cathedral and the noble ruins of abbeys such as Llanthony, Tintern and Lamphey Palace contrast in their splendour with the neat symmetry of the local chapels. These were once packed with worshippers and rang loud with hymns. Today their congregations are smaller but alongside them new religious foundations are thriving. Stand in any Welsh village or township on a Thursday, Saturday or Sunday evening and you will hear the solo chant of the Bingo Caller as the devout heads bowed in reverent silence gaze down at their little Book of Numbers. Then, piercing the silence, an ecstatic shout of 'Hallelujah' or 'House' can be heard. Visitors are welcome to join in as membership can usually be arranged at short notice.

Some of the most interesting buildings of their type found throughout Wales—such as chapels, farmhouses, woollen mills and pigsties—have been reconstructed at St. Fagan's Folk Museum, not far from Cardiff. But far more authentic are the typical workers' dwellings to be seen at such places as Dyffryn near Cardiff, Tredegar Park in Newport or Cyfarthfa Castle outside Merthyr. Here you will be struck by the ordered simplicity of the collier's neat cottage or the frugal homeliness of the ironworker's abode.

Where to stay

Wales offers the whole range of tourist accommodation—from modern guest-houses to plush hostelries. For those who want the luxury of a five-star hotel why not rent an apartment in one of the recently built Council offices that adorn the depressed area of Wales. In the holiday season you can stay in the Chief Executive's suite with its self-contained bathroom facilities and well-equipped cocktail cabinet. The Chief Officer will be pleased to arrange his schedule of meetings to fit in with your holiday plans so that he will only need to pop in occasionally to empty his in-tray (most Chief Exeutives nowadays are house-trained). His secretary will be on hand to make you cups of tea. A reduced tariff is available if you stay in the rooms of the other heads of departments. VAT is not normally charged but you will have to pay rates.

At the other end of the scale is the seaside guest-house. Make sure you read the rules of the house carefully. Breakfast, for example, is

normally served at a time when you would not usually be up for work, let alone on holiday. Facing a plate of tinned tomatoes floating on bacon fat may not be everyone's idea of a good start to the day, and since the breakfast menu remains the same all week, those with a delicate constitution may prefer to have a lie-in until nine a.m. when the knock on the door heralds the arrival of bed-making time.

Guests are usually allowed to stay out as late as nine p.m. on weekdays, with a half-hour extension on Saturdays for good behaviour. Guest houses are not licensed for alcoholic drinks, and in the more temperate zones you may have to take a breath test before being allowed in.

While it is not true that the Welsh live in caves, many of them at the height of the holiday season live in their own garages and let their houses out to tourists. Some owners offer a truly family holiday where you can share a house with mum, dad, the four kids and grandma. Or if this becomes too crowded you can camp out in the backyard at a reduced rate.

Yes, Wales, the land of song, welcomes you. 'We'll keep a welcome in the hillside, we'll keep a welcome in the vales'—but don't come after Christmas, we'll be busy with the sales.

Useful tips

The following suggestions should help you get the most out of your visit to Wales:

1. Do not be offended if you should hear the Welsh language being spoken in shops, pubs and other places of interest. Although at one time there were moves to make conversing in the national tongue an offence other than between consenting adults in private, it is now acceptable for all persons who wish to speak Welsh to do so. The Welsh lanuage now has legal parity with English.

2. Look out for some rare and moribund species of creatures still to be found in this beautiful land:

    the political dodo: this quaint animal still dwells in congested areas of southern Wales. Doomed to eventual extinction, it has not yet adapted to the environment of a bilingual Wales. The astute visitor can observe the dodo clinging tenaciously to its fragile political branch uttering loud but largely unintelligible cries of 'Yah-boo'.

    the yuppy bird: although a recent visitor to the shores of Wales, this migrant bird will probably not be nesting for much longer. A late realisation that its new found habitat is not just a suburb of Surbiton has led experts to conclude that it was probably blown off course during the recent spate of high winds and interest rates.

    the miner: driven out of its natural habitat over the years, this resilient creature has sought to adapt to a changing environment. Official hunters have systematically killed off this dying breed by cutting off alternative sources of sustenance.

3. If you are travelling by road be patient, especially if you are going via Builth Wells, Llandrindod Wells or Rhayader. Roads in this area of Wales were built by the Romans for their chariot Grand Prix—hence the number of sharp bends every fifty yards. In the peak holiday season traffic moves so slowly that you can pick blackberries as you drive along.

4. Be prepared for the weather. Wales is a

mountainous country and there is a good deal of rain. If you are staying in a guest house or rural hotel, look for the tell-tale signs of moss on the carpet and toadstools on the walls before you pay the deposit. Sou'westers and wellies are recommended beach-wear and may be hired along with covered deck-chairs and reinforced steel wind-breaks.

5. Visitors should appreciate that there is a strong non-conformist tradition in Wales. Consequently, there are very few naturist beaches. Nude bathing is only permitted for the under fives and grown females may only appear topless with the special permission of the local leisure and amenities committee. Application forms, to be completed in triplicate, can be obtained from the deck-chair attendant's hut.

6. Because of the chapel influence, tourists will find a number of temperance hotels and guest houses dotted throughout Wales. Frequented largely by retired persons and ex-Felinfoel drinkers, these establishments afford a restful sanctuary for visitors. Different social activities are arranged every weekday evening and range from silent beetle drives to the famous yard-of-Ovaltine drinking contest.

7. Local customs apply in some of the interesting markets which are to be found in all corners of Wales. In the Cardigan area, for example, stall-holders barter with the customers to increase the asking price. Using

one of the many excellent Basic Guides to Welsh, why not learn something of the language and try it out in the local market. Some errors may creep in and the occasional visitor has had to hire a trailer to take home the odd sheep or two after mistakenly believing they had bought a pound of laver bread, but the results are usually well worth the effort.

8. Some useful words and phrases:

Tŷ bach—Toilet

A oes meddyg yn y tŷ?—Is there a doctor in the house?

A oes meddyg yn y tŷ bach?—Is there a doctor in the toilet?

Saith, deg ac un deg saith—Chicken chop suey, curried octopus and prawn crackers

Ble mae fy nhrowsus?—That was quite a party!

Symud dy din—Excuse me but you appear to be sitting on my towel

Mae'r cwrw yma'n rhy wan—There's beer in my water

Arafwch nawr—Beware of police radar traps

A oes heddwch?—Can you keep the noise down please?

Canolfan Siopa—Lunatic Asylum

Gorsedd y Beirdd—Transvestites

Ble mae'r gwaith carthffosiaeth?—Where's the beach?

Llwybr Cyhoeddus—Public Footpath

Llwybr Preifat—Beware of the Bull

Rwy'n gwrando ar Stondin Sulwyn—I have a headache

Oes gennych chi ganiatâd cynllunio?—No sandcastles allowed

Rwyf eisiau llyfu pen-ôl y frenhines—I would like a first-class stamp

Mae'r mul yma yn uniaith Gymraeg—This donkey is deaf

Rwyf yn sgrechian—Ice Cream

Dim Ysmygu—Keep off the grass

Creigiau Presely—Elvis rocks!

Rwy'n cefnogi tim rygbi Castell Nedd—Call an ambulance!

Carchar—Holiday camp

Iechyd da—Cancel the ambulance

Ble mae'r archfarchnad?—Do you sell anything apart from coffins?

CLWYD

What a county of contrasts! The truly international mecca of North Wales, where people from all quarters of the globe come to perform, to holiday and to live.

ABERGELE

Now bypassed by the notorious A55 coast road—a boon for tourists and criminals—Abergele's traffic problems have been eased somewhat. The town is halfway between Rhyl and Colwyn Bay on what is commonly referred to as 'the North Wales Riviera', but is actually a mile from the sea. Sandy beaches and caravan parks are the order of the day on the shore but Abergele itself is laden with historical buildings. A mile to the west of the town is Gwrych Castle, an imposing mock antique building. If you are travelling by train, get off at Pensarn station—this is the nearest to the town. Also close by is the settlement at Towyn, which hit the headlines in the eighties after the sea breached the wall which was supposed to keep it at bay. For once, all the brochures proclaiming guest-houses with sea views and positions 'only two minutes from the sea' were telling the whole truth.

BRENIG RESERVOIR *(Llyn Brenig)*

High in the Hiraethog hills between Denbigh and Cerrigydrudion is Llyn Brenig. Winding roads have been upgraded into a wide open racetrack where cars towing power boats and bearing 'windsurfers do it standing up' stickers are the main tell-tale signs that Brenig isn't a natural lake. But engineers have done their best to persuade everyone that it is—the dam itself is a vast sloping affair hidden by thousands of tons of gently graded soil covered in that unnaturally green grass which is also evident in the South Wales valleys growing where the slag heaps used to be (and, somewhere underneath the lush growth, still are).

CORWEN

The Owain Glyndŵr Hotel in the centre of this small market town bears testimony to Corwen's connection with the famous Welsh rebel. Five miles away in the village of Glyndyfrdwy which gave him his name, was one of his estates, while his better-known property at Sycharth is south-east over the Berwyn mountains. An old legend also purports that a cross engraved on a stone lintel above the door of the local church was caused by a dagger thrown by Owain in a fit of ill-temper from a nearby mountain-top. Those with an interest in the past will also derive great pleasure from the remains—on another local mountain—of a prehistoric fortress. However, no one seems quite sure to what race it should be attributed.

DENBIGH (Dinbych)

Many guide books have described Denbigh as a rural town where sheep provide the main income. This is inaccurate—if you don't believe me, visit the place and count how many sheep you spot buying anything. The castle ruins, which stand in an imposing position on a hill in the centre of the town, are not the town's best-known building—that title must go to the local psychiatric hospital. But the town can boast to being the birthplace of at least two famous Welshmen—one a name known throughout Wales, another throughout the world. Twm o'r Nant was an eighteenth-century playwright regarded as the Welsh Shakespeare (which some would claim as being rather nasty to Twm). The other was Henry Morton Stanley, who uttered those immortal words 'Dr. Livingstone, I presume?' in the middle of the jungle. Considering that they were probably the only white men in Africa at the time, it was a pretty fair assumption.

HOLYWELL (Treffynnon)

This old Flintshire town overlooking the Dee estuary was named after a well which sprang up at the spot where *Santes Gwenffrewi* (St Winefride) literally lost her head while stoutly defending her virginity from a lustful gentleman by the name of Caradog. Such species are now very thin on the ground in the area.

LLANGOLLEN

Every year the International Eisteddfod is held in this quaint little town. Welsh choirs, dancers and soloists rarely win, which makes the National Eisteddfod (see text) even more important. Llangollen Bridge, consisting of four unequal pointed arches, is listed among the Seven Wonders of Wales and crosses a picturesque section of the Shropshire Union Canal. At Pontcysyllte near the town is Thomas Telford's aqueduct, a cast iron trough supported on eighteen stone pillars that carries the canal at a height of 200 feet above the Dee Valley.

MOLD *(Yr Wyddgrug)*

This is the administrative centre of Clwyd. The painter Richard Wilson and the writer Daniel Owen both have strong connections with the County town and it has its own theatre company. Speculation about the origin of the town's name have occupied scholars over the years. Could it be a corruption of *Moel* (hill) or *Moled* (kerchief), or did some illiterate anglophile leave the middle 'u' out?

RHUDDLAN

Lying on the river Clwyd, Rhuddlan's attraction lies mainly in its castle, although it is a much more pleasant place to be than nearby Rhyl. It was at the castle that the forces of Offa (famous for his Dyke) inflicted a terrible massacre on the massed Welsh army, and to commemorate it several centuries later, the Welsh did one of the two things that they always do on such dark occasions—in the absence of the almost compulsory poet, they composed a melody called *Morfa Rhuddlan* (the Marsh of Rhuddlan).

RHYL

The English translation is 'Eastbourne'. This seaside resort has attracted many visitors to return permanently to live in their retirement homes creating a little England beyond England. What makes Rhyl so specially attractive? Perhaps it's the fabulous Sun Centre with its built-in surprise—there's a roof over it to protect you from the sun's harmful rays!—a sort of 'Absence of Sun Centre'.

RUTHIN *(Rhuthun)*

In the delightful Vale of Clwyd stands Ruthin Castle. Once a mediaeval fortress it is now a luxury hotel. Family dungeons are available but at luxury prices; it was probably easier to get into the original castle.

ST. ASAPH (Llanelwy)

A few miles south of Rhuddlan lies the city of St. Asaph, which boasts the smallest cathedral in Wales and also the plainest, as if in silent tribute to the austere way of life of the early Christians. Outside is a monument to Bishop William Morgan, William Salesbury, Bishop Richard Davies and Thomas Huet who together were responsible for translating both the Old and New Testament into Welsh in the mid sixteenth century. Like Denbigh, the town boasts connections with the sharp-minded explorer Henry Morton Stanley—and for some reason the local hospital is named after him.

WREXHAM (Wrecsam)

A fine mix of architecture here, ranging from traditional Nondescript to modern Featurelessness. This unique town was recently the epicentre of an earthquake. This was remarkable since only two weeks previously Wrexham had been nominated by its inhabitants as 'The place we would most like to be the epicentre of an earthquake'.

To be fair, Wrexham Steeple, the tower of St Giles' Parish Church, is listed as the second of the Seven Wonders of Wales and remains the dominant feature of the town's skyline. A replica of the steeple has been constructed into the university buildings of Yale, Connecticut, which accounts for the crowds of camera-clad American tourists who flock to Wrexham every year. There is also a football stadium here, next door to an American High School style further education college.

DYFED

Some may say that this county serves as the cultural and academic centre of Wales with its university towns, its ecclesiastical sites and Llanelli—yes, Llanelli. What other nation of bards could pen a stirring slogan to arms—with such defiant lines as: 'The little saucepan is boiling on the fire' and 'The cat has scratched little Johnny'!

ABERAERON

Many guide books have striven to describe Aberaeron without using the adjective 'pretty'. Most have failed and this one is no exception. 'Pretty' would appear to be an euphemism for 'well-planned': Aberaeron is one of the few examples in Wales of a town which was built to a set plan. It was developed in the early nineteenth century and most of the houses around the harbour favour the Regency style, which was all the rage at the time. By today, they seem to be the basis for a local friendly-neighbourly competition to establish who can paint their external walls in the most vivid colour. Daffodil yellow, subdued greens and garish pinks and magentas are the undoubted favourites—thus forming a clear contrast with the brown silt of the harbour when the tide is out.

ABERYSTWYTH

A university by the sea stands here and the National Library of Wales (the magnificent casino-like building overlooking the town) which keeps a copy of every book in print.

Like so many other beaches in Wales, there are hazards for those tourists who enjoy splashing about in the sea. Four flags fly on the sand, each one giving a different message. Flag 1: 'Safe bathing for those equipped with a wet suit, diver's helmet and an underdeveloped sense of smell.'; Flag 2: 'Avoid bathing unless you wish to emerge from the water looking as though you have just acquired an instant tan.'; Flag 3: 'Not advised unless your sense of fun is bobsleighing through sewage pipes.'; Flag 4: 'The sea is so dirty even the waves won't come in.'

To compensate for the lack of swimming, Aberystwyth has to try that much harder to please the tourists. There are nearly fifty pubs and a smattering of ancient relics—the castle, the pier and several of the human variety who have struggled across the road to sit on the promenade in their striped deckchairs (the pubs are almost outnumbered by old people's homes).

Aberystwyth tries hard to please tourists.

Treasure hunters at Aberystwyth.

In summer, it's possible to play an interesting game—find the parking space. Unfortunately there are few winners. One building on the sea-front was knocked down to build a car park. That just about sums the place up, although it has a mysterious appeal to former students who are drawn back there like pins to a magnet.

BORTH

Like the stoat and the ermine, Borth is a different animal in summer and winter. Built on a narrow arm of solid ground with the sea on one side and a vast bog on the other, summer sees the village groaning under the weight of full caravan parks with the sandy beach hidden from view by a multitude of brightly-coloured beach blankets and sun-screens. Water-skiing is popular, but the 'in' sports in high summer are seeking shelter from torrential thunderstorms and guessing when the power supply is going to be cut. It is rumoured that surplus wax from the candles used in Borth during any given year could keep Madame Tussaud's turning over for a good few months.

In winter, however, it's a different story. Since most of the houses are second homes (all are sold with a box of candles and sandbags thrown in), the main street in December resembles Dodge City when the James brothers were in town. Everyone seems unwilling to ven-

Borth—closed for the winter.

ture outside in case they are swept away by the oft-anticipated (but so far mythical) 'freak wave'. Businessmen with an eye for a fast buck would be well advised to open a shop selling 'Closed' signs.

CARDIGAN *(Aberteifi)*

Despite the opening of a recent bypass to avoid the town, Cardigan is well worth a visit, if only to explore its quaint one-way system. Confused visitors will often swear blind that the town has at least three castles, but don't be fooled—it's only the same one, but it seems to change places (visitors to London will experience the same phenomenon with the Telecom Tower—wherever you go you're able to see it, until you're eventually convinced that there are two of them. Try finding the spot where it meets the ground and you'll agree that it's easier to locate the end of the rainbow). After driving round and round for a few miles, head for the beach at Mwnt—apart from a church, a car park and some sand, there's nothing there—but after several circular tours of Cardigan, anything looks good.

CARMARTHEN *(Caerfyrddin)*

This is a market town with fine castle walls that once protected a Welsh princess. The old legend is fascinating and says that if the old oak tree that stood for centuries in the town should ever fall, then Carmarthen would sink into the sea. Not long ago the decrepit tree was removed. Since then, Wrexham has suffered an earthquake, Towyn in North Wales has been flooded and Cardiff City have been relegated to Division Four. The tree must have had hellish long roots.

DEVIL'S BRIDGE *(Pontarfynach)*

Just as the names of Stockton and Darlington are inseparable to the railway fraternity in the north of England, so are Aberystwyth and Devil's Bridge in Wales. The Vale of Rheidol steam-line has its eastern terminus at this small village, which is ten miles from Aberystwyth by road. But the journey on the narrow-gauge track is much more spectacular, as it clings to the wooded sides of the Rheidol valley. When you get there, follow all the other passengers to witness the one thing which sets Devil's Bridge apart from the other local villages. Unlike Conwy in Gwynedd, it doesn't boast a castle. However it can match Conwy's three bridges—and one of them might even rival Telford's technical achievements. All three are above each other, crossing a narrow gorge where the river Mynach meets the Rheidol—the upper two being the old road bridge and, above it, the new one. The lowest dates back to the Middle Ages and gives the village it's Welsh name—*Pontarfynach*.

Built by the monks of Strata Florida Abbey, Devil's Bridge seems strangely inappropriate. But the nearby waterfalls form a seething cauldron of fierce white water known as the Devil's Punchbowl—a name which is a little more understandable.

FISHGUARD (Abergwaun)

The setting for the film *Under Milk Wood* in 1971, this port is busy throughout the year, but particularly on those biennial occasions when Welsh rugby supporters cross the sea to Ireland. On those days the small streets are alive with red and white scarves and faces like semi-mobile Toby Jugs make their way to the ferries believing they have arrived at Holyhead.

It was here that a French force landed with nearly 1400 troops. The purpose of the invasion in 1797 has never really been clarified. Some historians say that they were blown off course on their way to Ireland but there is no record of a rugby international having been arranged in that year. Whatever the reason, the French invaders were beaten back by a hastily marshalled group of locals who repelled the French by brandishing large leeks and singing some very early Dafydd Iwan recordings.

HAVERFORDWEST (Hwlffordd)

It is often claimed in Wales that the last bastions of the Welsh language are firmly entrenched on the western coast. The majority of the old county of Pembrokeshire *(Sir Benfro)* is the exception that proves the rule. Basking in the dubious glory of the title 'Little England beyond Wales', Haverfordwest is, to all intents and purposes, a bastion of Englishness. To the north of the town runs a Welsh equivalent to the Equator—the Landsker, an invisible line which divides the Welsh-speaking north of the county from the anglicised south, the onset of which is attributed to the Norman invasion which had much the same effect in the Vale of Glamorgan—supplanting the traditional Welsh place-names with English replacements. Tavernspite, Saundersfoot, Broadhaven and Bosherston are ideal examples.

LAMPETER (Llanbedr Pont Steffan)

Another university town with a college that was once dedicated exclusively to theological studies. Described in other tourist guides as 'busy and bustling', it is about as busy as a chapel on a Monday and as bustling as a pub with no beer. This all changes however when there's a sale at B. J. Jones. Renowned throughout the world—well, west Wales anyway—for its fashions, it has been called 'the Harrods of Wales'. Some have suggested that is because only Arabs can afford to shop there. This is patently untrue since Audi-driving farmers' wives flock there to buy a little something for the Farmers Union of Wales dinner, the Council bash or a soirée at the Mayor's residence. The current recession in farming has made a difference though—they now drive there in their P-registration Land Rovers.

LLANDEILO

This market town in the Tywi valley attracts many tourists simply because of its location. Residents of Hereford and Shropshire headed for the rugged coastlines and golden beaches of south-west Wales pass through on the roads from Builth Wells and Brecon, but rarely stop to sample the delights that the area holds. But if they are attracted by such things as golden beaches, chances are that the ruined castle of Carreg Cennen, the ruined abbey at Talyllychau and the remains of Roman gold-mining operations at Dolau Cothi would hardly make them draw in a wistful breath. Llandeilo doesn't boast a golden beach—or any other sort of beach for that matter—but the fact that something is different doesn't necessarily make it a bad thing. And you can still buy sun-cream and ice-cream there . . .

LLANDOVERY (Llanymddyfri)

Like Llandeilo, Llandovery is a Tywi valley market town which has a great passing trade in tourists. Local attract-

ions are very similar to those of Llandeilo too—mainly because the two towns are only about twelve miles apart. But Llandovery has one added claim—the nearby birthplace of arguably the greatest Welsh hymnwriter, William Williams, Pantycelyn. Oddly enough, the town is also noted for its profusion of public houses. A charter by Richard III designated it as the only one throughout the area which had the right to establish taverns. And if public houses are the order of the day, why not a public school too? Llandovery can lay claim to one of those as well—who says that private education and drunken debauchery don't go hand in hand?

LLANELLI

One of the few remaining towns in the south where the Welsh language has not slipped into quiet anonimity, and most of the non-Welsh speakers can manage to recite one verse of a traditional song. That is *Sosban Fach*—the little saucepan. In a country noted for its rigid Nonconformism, Llanelli is a town where the old order is threatened by the all-consuming passion which is . . . rugby. And the saucepan has become a symbol which bears as much significance in Llanelli as the daffodil or leek. On a Saturday afternoon, the voices of the massed ranks on the terraces at Stradey Park *(Parc y Strade)* echo all around the town, and a pair of saucepans on top of the rugby posts at either end of the ground are a constant reminder of where you are. Even during the week, when a return to normality would be expected, much of the street talk is of rugby—all against a background of ever-present scarlet and white.

LLANGRANNOG

A small Ceredigion coastal village which is the location of one of the main Urdd activity camps (see section on Urdd Eisteddfod). The atmosphere is somewhere between scouts, girl guides and Stalag 17. There are other encampments nearby, remains of other Celtic and Roman habitations and what might seem at first sight to be Apache reservations. There are the tepees of the 'happy hippies', a nationless breed who have chosen Wales as their haven from anything to do with civilisation. Their camps are usually sited just near enough to the local Social Security offices where they reluctantly hurry each Monday to collect their state benefits.

If they subscribe to the motto 'All play and no work', one of the village's famous daughters certainly didn't. Suffragette Sarah Jane Rees (alias Cranogwen) was a real bundle of fun. Not content with promoting the teaching of tonic sol-fa, she also founded a temperance movement for the women of South Wales.

NANT-Y-MOCH

The reservoir at Nant-y-moch is one of those rare specimens in Wales—it wasn't built to supply water to England. It nevertheless drowned one of the few remaining Welsh wildernesses and used all the arguments prevalent in such cases—'it'll look nice', 'we'll build new roads', 'anything's better than acres of nothing'. Those 'acres of nothing' include the mountain of Hyddgen, near which Owain Glyndŵr's army gained a famous victory over the troops of Henry IV . . .

NEWCASTLE EMLYN (Castellnewydd Emlyn)

Newcastle Emlyn is a small market town standing on the Teifi river, which formed the boundary between the old counties of Cardiganshire and Carmarthenshire. The village of Adpar, separated from the town only by a bridge, lays claim to being the location of the first printing press in Wales, while more of the country's old traditions are still alive (but not exactly kicking) in nearby Cenarth. There, some still scrape a livelihood through fishing by coracle—small round boats steered with a stick. It looks easy, but the uninitiated can spend hours going round in circles. Talking of which, Cardigan is only a few miles away . . .

NEW QUAY (Ceinewydd)

It's fair to say that most visitors to West Wales will want to see New Quay before they return home. It's also fair to say that New Quay will want to see most visitors to West Wales. Blatantly touristified—caravan parks, holiday parks, hotels and guest-houses multiply at a greater rate of knots than the proverbial rabbits—the village seems to have been transferred brick by brick from Cornwall, where quaint cliffside fishing villages have their natural habitat. Pack the usual holiday accessories, but leave one case aside for crampons, ropes and climbing boots—those streets are steep! And if you do own some kind of boat, the harbour should be your Mecca—the only problem being finding a vacant patch of sea on which to float it.

PEMBROKE (Penfro)

A lovely settlement with a magnificent castle and close to fine beaches. Even when the old county of Pembrokeshire was 'dry' it still maintained the highest rate of drunkenness in the whole of Wales. A boost to its economy and ethnic diversity came with the German Panzer Divisions for military training. They have now been here for many years. Last year's Chairman of Rotary was local boy—Fritz von Wilhelm ap Robat.

THE PEMBROKESHIRE COAST NATIONAL PARK *(Parc Cenedlaethol Arfordir Sir Benfro)*

A thin strip of coastal path that guides the walker along beautiful vistas of sea and rocks. Wildlife abounds on the offshore islands for they are home to a variety of less familiar birds; the razorbill, the puffin and the fulmar. Tranquility is all around so if you are walking along the cliff's edge and chance to meet another hiker carrying a blaring radio-cassette player, give him a little nudge. There are always birds of prey circling around who will be glad you did.

Its coves and unspoilt beaches offer a rare opportunity for those tourists who prefer a certain solitude. Visitors who prefer the experience of complete strangers sitting on their towel with a brood of noisome offspring and an incontinent dog would probably prefer Barmouth or Barry Island.

Naturally the Armed Forces have been attracted to this quiet corner of West Wales. So not far from the delightful beaches of Barafundle and Broadhaven, military enthusiasts can go tank-spotting near the Castlemartin Army Ranges. At Brawdy, the RAF have long had their base. Locals now expect the arrival any day of a flotilla of destroyers to sail peacefully overnight into Fishguard Harbour.

PENDINE *(Pentywyn)*

If your idea of a good holiday is to live amongst hundreds of caravans nestling 'twixt a cluster of souvenir shops and a military barracks, this is the place for you. Pendine has a unique aura about it caused largely by the fall-out from weapons' testing. On the long flat sands many an attempt has been made on the land speed record and it is still true that most visitors leave Pendine a good deal faster than they arrived.

PRESELY *(Y Preselau)*

The Presely hills in north Pembrokeshire possess an undeniably mystical quality—quite apart from being often shrouded in mist! Monuments and relics literally litter the slopes—the cromlech at Pentre Ifan possibly being the best-known. But the Presely is also associated with the rites of the ancient druids—not the modern Eisteddfod variety—in another less famous way. Geological surveyors have proved beyond a shadow of a doubt that the stones used to build Stonehenge in Wiltshire came from one outcrop in the area. But it's obvious at once that they left plenty behind them. Near the small village of Mynachlog-ddu there lies a Son of Stonehenge—a stone circle on a smaller scale than the Wiltshire version but essentially serving the same purpose.

ST DAVID'S *(Tyddewi)*

The presence of arguably the most spectacular of Welsh cathedrals in the village fuels its vigorous claim to the title of 'the smallest city in Wales'. Even then, there seems to have been an earnest attempt to hide it. Situated in a small hollow, only the tower is visible from the village until you get close—then the magnificent sandstone structure appears before you as if from nowhere. The nave contains the shrine of St David, but the magnificently preserved cathedral—the third to be built on the site—contrasts sharply with the surrounding buildings. Little more than the walls of the Bishop's Palace and the tall battlements of St Mary's College have stood the test of time. And that, as they say, is that. There is precious little else in the 'city' to keep you occupied—unless visiting tea rooms turns you on.

STRATA FLORIDA *(Ystrad-fflur)*

The abbey of Strata Florida—the way of flowers—has been referred to as 'the Westminster of Wales'. There ends any further similarity. The roof is long gone, as are most of the walls, and the cross-shape formed by the outer walls is only barely visible. Not surprising when you consider that it was once struck by lightning, and burned by Edward I when attempting to impose his authority over the Welsh nationalists. A curious twist from current events. Tradition has it that the great Welsh poet and troubadour Dafydd ap Gwilym is buried in the shadow of a yew tree within its grounds.

TENBY *(Dinbych-y-pysgod)*

This picturesque walled town offers the holidaymaker a wide variety of activities. There is a fine harbour, two sandy beaches and a mediaeval atmosphere about the streets and some notable buildings such as the Tudor Merchant's House. One or two restaurants actually prepare meals in which chips are not obligatory. Reservations are not necessary. Perhaps the most appealing feature about Tenby is that it is not Pendine.

Not far from Tenby is the Oakwood Leisure Park which has won a few tourist awards. Go-karts and bobsleighs are large enough to accommodate adults, so leave the kids in the car and enjoy yourselves. At last, a non-ageist fun centre where you may see octogenarians tackling the assault course and grandma and grandad eating ice-creams as they enjoy their tenth ride on the rollercoaster. Lost false teeth can be reclaimed at the site caravan, and entry to the 'wall of death' is open to everyone on the production of a valid pension book. The Park has an excellent safety record. So far there have only been a few minor accidents such as exploding girdles and torn gussets. These have been dealt with promptly by the resident team of paramedics and corset restorers.

One fascinating corner of the museum is set aside to re-create the familiar sounds and scenery of Wales—from the raucous cry of seagulls as they dip into Tenby harbour to the crunch of pigeons underfoot on Hayes Island. Here, indeed, is another tourist attraction. Hayes Island is a bird sanctuary surrounded by water (the local name is 'urinals'). Ferries to the island leave every hour from Cardiff docks but the voyage can be a little choppy, especially in the pedestrianised area. There is a snack bar on the island and a kiosk where you can buy tickets for the local lottery known as 'spot the bus'.

TREGARON

Hidden deep in the heart of the barren inland hills of West Wales, the town of Tregaron retains its Welsh character despite having to some extent borne the brunt of immigration from England. The area's numerous smallholdings are like a magnet to disillusioned city dwellers who like the idea of escaping from the rat-race. It doesn't help their cause when they suddenly discover that they don't know one end of a sheep from another. Organic vegetables and goat's cheese abound in local shops.

The town is, rather unfortunately, best known for the four square mile bog to the north, but it does boast two

famous sons. The obligatory statue to one of them, Henry Richard, stands in the town's main square. He was known as the 'Apostle of Peace' for his work with the Peace Union, the Victorian forerunner of the United Nations. Peace was not high on the list of interests of the other—Thomas Jones, or Twm Siôn Cati, a sixteenth-century highwayman and bandit who plied his trade in a locale which spread as far as Llandovery to the south. Highway robbery has now been replaced by blatant overcharging on such salubrious items as organic vegetables and goat's cheese.

GWENT

Gwent, in the east of South Wales, is a somewhat schizophrenic county but all the more charming because of it. The rugged, stark landscapes of the industrial valleys contrast with the more gentle, lush slopes of eastern Gwent. There, on the borders of England, lie the picturesque settlements of Monmouth, Usk, Abergavenny and Chepstow. The sport here is good; if you are lucky, you could catch a salmon or even a Welsh accent.

ABERGAVENNY *(Y Fenni)*
This pleasant market town in the Usk valley basks in the title of the 'Gateway to Wales', which is rooted deep in the historical fact that most English invasions of Wales were centred on this area. By today, it's difficult to tell that you're in Wales at all. Standing in the shadow of four strangely-named mountains—the Skirrid, the Little Skirrid, the Sugar Loaf and Blorenge—the dearth of Welsh-speakers makes it difficult to believe that during the last century the town was an important centre in a growing movement to revive traditional Welsh culture. This was mainly due to the efforts of Lord and Lady Llanover, but when the lord passed away, so did the

annual eisteddfod, which drew the cream of Welsh literatti to the area.

Now the town is best known as the starting (or finishing) point of the infamous Heads of the Valleys road leading to Swansea—so named because it runs just north of all the famous South Wales mining valleys.

CAERLEON *(Caerllion)*

This is a Roman encampment a few miles from Newport. This village has an amphitheatre, a barracks and a museum. Tennyson stayed here in his quest for knowledge about the Arthurian legend. In fact, Caerleon has probably the largest number of pubs per square metre in Wales plus a Tandoori restaurant. This was obviously the real reason why Tennyson and Caesar's lads decided to come here in the first place.

CHEPSTOW *(Cas-gwent)*

Since the opening of the Severn Bridge, Chepstow, previously the most southerly entry point into Wales, is only held in high regard by the horse-racing fraternity. The Welsh Grand National is run here annually, drawing thousands of that curious breed who are ready and willing to put their shirts (and blouses for that matter) on a temperamental and rarely trustworthy beast.

CWMBRÂN

Five miles north of Newport lies Cwmbrân—an example of that much-heralded concept of the new way of life, the new town. The main characteristics of a new town are well-planned streets and estates, acres of car parking space, millions of unsightly bricks and a vehicle-free town centre. When you have parked your car, you discover the catch—apart form a largely-empty athletics stadium, there's absolutely nothing else there. If you're one of those people who have great difficulty in finding enough white space on the back of a post-card to describe all the sights, take note—Cwmbrân's vehicle-free town centre is crammed with people in trances trying to scrape together enough material to fill up the white space on the back of a stamp.

EBBW VALE *(Glynebwy)*

Sightseers have mainly steered away from the bright lights of Ebbw Vale; the sightseers were right. Another of the South Wales coal-mining communities which has had its heart ripped out of it, the town and valley are perhaps most famous for being the parliamentary constituency of the late Aneurin Bevan, who founded the National Health Service (which, by strange coincidence, has also had its heart ripped out). Local unemployment is high, although most of those who find themselves out of work still manage to dress better than present MP Michael Foot.

MONMOUTH *(Trefynwy)*

The only people to whoop and screech with excitement in Monmouth are architecture buffs. Apart from that, there's really little to raise the temperature here. You shouldn't really expect much of any town which is most famous for its bridge—even though it is quite a bridge, complete with a stone arch you have to pass through to enter the town, or, for that matter, to leave.

NEWPORT *(Casnewydd-ar-Wysg)*

How can a town of over 134,000 inhabitants be described as 'sleepy'? Why not go to Newport and find out. On a still day, the collective snores of the elected worthies can be heard wafting from the civic centre housed in buildings of the post-war mausoleum style.

The more intrepid tourist can leap onto the top of High Street Bridge and abseil down to see a bit of a wall that once belonged to the castle. Very little information can be found about the history of this noble pile of rubble. Mischievous Cardiffians will tell you that it was built not to keep enemies at bay but to stop its citizens from getting out.

Newport's claim to fame is its association with the Chartists. It was here outside the Westgate Hotel that the militia fired upon a group of agitators who had marched down 5,000 strong. Their leader, John Frost, addressed his followers in Welsh. But more recently the denizens of Newport have had to ask themselves some puzzling questions: Are we Welsh or are we English? Do we live in Gwent or in Monmouthshire? Will our rugby team ever win a game?

Newport has excellent road communications until you get to the Severn Bridge. On most weekends and Bank Holidays, this engineering conundrum enables you to cross from Wales to England in twice the time it would have taken you if you had gone via Gloucester or even via Edinburgh. It is a curious anachronism. Constructed in the era of lunar exploration, it was originally built in order to accommodate four lanes of traffic but over the years the lanes have narrowed to the extent that it will barely take two horses and carts. Five years from now—assuming it has not vanished into the sea—visitors travelling from the English side would be well advised to leave the cart behind and, if possible, the horse as well.

The toll has always been a contentious issue in Wales, erupting in the Rebecca riots in 1839 when more than 100 tollgates were destroyed because of the financial hardship laid upon farmers. Quite recently the toll to cross the Severn Bridge has doubled but is still wonderful value compared with prices in the nearby services complex. Here payment by Access is accepted for a portion of tomato ketchup.

PONTYPOOL *(Pont-y-pŵl)*

Those of you who treasure memories of hidden moments in the back row of the cinema really should be prepared before venturing into Pontypool, otherwise you'll think that their cinematic experiences were strangely different. Don't be surprised if you hear all the locals reminiscing about the golden days of the Pontypool Front Row, but make sure that you know the facts first. The famed 'Front Row' were three burly rugby players, Charlie Faulkner, Bobby Windsor and Graham Price, who became legends in the seventies both locally and by playing for Wales when the whole team were household names. Since then the fortunes of the local and national rugby teams, as well as those of the town itself, have suffered quite a dive.

RAGLAN *(Rhaglan)*

Another of those numerous Welsh towns which owe their fame to their castles—this one was the last to hold out against Parliament in the First Civil War—Raglan lies in the vast emptiness of countryside between Monmouth and Pontypool. Two kings of England are reputed to have spent some time at the castle—though this is no recommendation. Charles I was a guest after his defeat at the Battle of Naseby, and Henry VII, before acceding to the throne, was held prisoner there. It might take a cell to persuade you to stay too.

TINTERN *(Tyndyrn)*

A spot immortalized by Wordsworth as he and his sister paused on their journey to the nearest Chinese takeaway. Amid the ruins of this former Cistercian House, the visitor is left to speculate about the spartan simplicity of the devoted monks or conjecture as to how may semis Wimpey could build on a nicely levelled site.

GWYNEDD

The most resistently Welsh-speaking area of Wales despite countless invasions symbolised by the presence of impressive castles ('An Englishman's home is his castle') and a minor aberration when Ynys Môn returned an English public schoolboy as its MP. Only the castles remain ...

BANGOR

A cathedral town situated at the eastern entrance to the Menai Strait, Bangor boasts a fine University College—perhaps the most Welsh of all the Colleges in Wales. Atop the building flies the Union Jack, which says something about the other Welsh Colleges! The city itself is split into two sections, upper and lower. The former's population is made up entirely of students, who ensure that the pubs are constantly full. The area is quite cosmopolitan—local greengrocers make a roaring trade in guavas, lychees and mangoes. In the mountain settlements nearby, local people have never even seen a guava and most think a lychee is something local doctors use to suck blood from their patients.

Lower Bangor, as the name suggests, is lower.

Overlooked by the imperiously-sited university, students who choose to live there spend the first few hundred pounds of their grant on climbing equipment. Some say that if Berlin had been built on a site like Bangor's they wouldn't have needed to build a wall in the first place.

Bangor does boast a pier, even though it can hardly be classed as a resort. Unless it's a last resort that is. Visitors are reminded that there is another Bangor (*Is-coed* or *Bangor-on-Dee*). Here stood one of the earliest monasteries in Britain until the Saxons came to the area, putting many monks to the sword whilst the rest fled over the sea to Bardsey Island *(Ynys Enlli)*. The Saxons probably came to complain about the tatty souvenirs sold to them by the monks during their previous visit and were given short shrift (if you'll excuse the expression) by the holy brothers when they asked for their money back.

Nowadays the tradition of purveying pap is carried on by the monks who inhabit Caldey Island which is across the water from Tenby in the west of Wales (see entry for 'Tenby')

Y BALA

Chiefly noted for its lake (the largest natural lake in Wales), called, with a touch of curious irony, Bala Lake *(Llyn Tegid* in Welsh) and all the sports usually linked to such inland waters—sailing, water-skiing and windsurfing. Canoeing championships are often held on the Tryweryn river, which is fed to a foaming frenzy of white water by Liverpool's surplus requirements from the Tryweryn reservoir.

If there is a hint of Scottish in the curiously-named Loch Café on its shores, the town itself is all things Welsh. Statues to famous sons abound. Thomas Charles who founded the British and Foreign Bible Society after giving his personal Bible to Mary Jones, a young girl who had walked barefoot several miles to see him, is immortalised in stone outside a local chapel. But the prime site, on the tree-lined main street, is occupied by the memorial to T.I.Ellis, who became the Liberal MP for Meirionnydd in 1886 (beating famous Irish politician Charles Parnell for the nomination). Unfortunately, prime sites must accept prime hazards—dawn has broken on a Sunday morning several times only to reveal him in full glory, traffic cone on head, (empty) beer can in hand.

BARDSEY ISLAND *(Ynys Enlli)*

An old legend has it that 20,000 saints are buried on Bardsey—but judging by its size, most of them have been interred one on top of the other. Avid map readers will know that the island is at the head of the Llŷn Peninsula *(Pen Llŷn)*—but just you try finding it. As you approach the village of Aberdaron, you assume that it's 'just round the corner'. Several corners later, and still no sign of it, you'll begin to wonder whether it exists at all, or whether it's just another Welsh legend. But eventually, there it is—across the treacherous waters of the Swnt— unless of course it's misty.

BARMOUTH *(Abermo)*

Possibly the only town this side of the Andes to be built in a vertical fashion. Barmouth stands on the estuary of the Mawddach river and has glorious views of the Cader Idris range. If you're into sun, sand and sea, this is the place for you (well, two out of three ain't bad). If you're into architecture, you'd do well to stay away. The town isn't noted for its ancient monuments, apart from the blue-rinsed variety on the promenade benches. Swimming, particularly by the river mouth, is for avid lifeboat-spotters only.

BEAUMARIS *(Biwmares)*

The very name of this impressive fortified town bears witness to the Norman incursions throughout Wales. Here Edward I built a concentric castle in 1295 in his attempt to hold the Welsh in check. Strange how Roman, Norman and Teutonic invaders have found attacking Welsh people such an irresistible pastime over the centuries. It's true that Wales has been fortunate in holding such attractive natural resources as the gold-mine at Dolau Cothi, the slate quarries at Blaenau Ffestiniog and the laver-bread pits near Swansea testify.

Nowadays *Cymru* (Wales) gives a warm *croeso* (welcome) to much gentler marauders (tourists). Here in North Wales and indeed throughout the Principality (land of Llywelyn/Charles) the visitor can buy a keepsake as a sentimental souvenir, craft shops abound, selling uniquely Welsh items such as love-spoons, map of Wales tea-towels, tartan-like jackets worn almost exclusively by members of *Merched y Wawr* (see footnote) and, by special delivery, the world's largest confectionery—a stick of rock with Llanfair Pwllgwyngyll go-ger y chwyrndrobwll Llantysilio go-go-goch running all the way through it.

N.B. *Merched y Wawr* (Women of the Dawn): a coven of formidable Welsh matrons dedicated to the virtues of the hearth. Home-made wines a speciality.

BEDDGELERT

Nowhere but in Wales could a village have attained notoriety through a dog's grave. That is Beddgelert's one (if not only) claim to fame. The name itself means Gelert's Grave—which proves that it's all in a name. Beddfido just doesn't have the same ring to it. Countless

Barmouth (Abermo) is not noted for its architecture.

coaches every year draw the sentimental tourist there, intrinsically to shed a quiet tear and stare at a piece of stone standing in the middle of a field. The whole area is littered with so many such stones that they've put some iron railings around the supposed headstone—just in case you mourn in the wrong place.

To be fair, Gelert was no ordinary hound. He was Prince Llywelyn's best friend. Left in charge of the royal offspring one day, he saved the child from a marauding wolf (which are long since extinct in these parts, apart from one or two behind the counters of some of the village's myriad gift shops). On his return, Llywelyn mistook the blood and gore for the junior prince's remains and put poor Gelert to the sword. Prospective babysitters please note.

BETHESDA

The fictional Canadian-American border town of Twin Peaks has nothing on Bethesda, which nestles in the Ogwen valley amidst some of the highest mountains in Wales. Garnedd Llywelyn and Garnedd Dafydd (number two and three to Snowdon itself) are a stone's throw away—or should that be a slate's throw away. There are certainly plenty of them available to throw. If coal rubble is synonymous with the South Wales valleys, then slate rubble is the North's equivalent. Bethesda was home to

the famous Penrhyn slate quarry, and examples of its multi-coloured product—blue, green, grey and red—can be found the world over. Welsh chapel-goers are often accused of being rather dry—Penrhyn quarry slates are one of the contributary factors.

The positioning of Bethesda on the A5 trunk road can be explained in two ways, depending on which way you're heading. Travelling from Bangor, the Ogwen valley seems that much more beautiful with Bethesda behind you; travelling from the East, it brings you back down to earth.

BETWS-Y-COED

If you're heading towards Snowdonia from the Midlands, as thousands do, there's only one way to go—through Betws-y-coed. During high summer, the tortuous bends and narrow roads are packed with nose-to-tail cars and coaches. Many have suggested that this village is the prime reason for so many English people settling in North Wales—they just can't face going through it all again on the way back.

Local attractions include the much-vaunted Fairy Glen and the spectacular Swallow Falls *(Rhaeadr Ewynnol)*. Many tourists queue up and pay to see the waterfalls—not content with viewing Welsh water in captivity (bath night), they want to see it in its natural

habitat. Locals are much more blasé about it—some brave souls have even been known to canoe down the falls—hence their name.

BLAENAU FFESTINIOG

Blaenau Ffestiniog is the archetypal Welsh quarry town. Set high in the horseshoe created by the Moelwyn and Manod mountains, everything about it screams 'slate'. Houses, roofs, fences, paving stones—all made of slate, testifying to the far-off days when the industry and the area were prosperous. All that remains of the working ways of the quarrymen can be found at the town's two main tourist attractions—the Gloddfa Ganol Slate Mine and the Llechwedd Slate Caverns. Both offer the usual array of facilities—traditional cafés, restaurants, olde worlde pubs, craft workshops and, rather ironically when you consider the stunning scenery all around, underground tours. If agoraphobia is not on your list of ills, you'll also enjoy a trip on the Ffestiniog narrow gauge railway. Built originally to ferry slates to Porthmadog for export, it now caters for importing tourists.

A note for sun-seekers. The town dubiously enjoys a status equivalent to that of Manchester in England—the Welsh capital of rainfall. But still not enough to make it suitable for boating holidays.

CAERNARFON

Not since 1282 has there been a Prince of Wales. However, in 1969 a re-creation was staged in the castle by a now forgotten Hollywood producer and the spectacle gained a worldwide audience. The leading actor and supporting cast have rarely been seen since.

In spite of this, Caernarfon still reigns supreme as North Wales' media capital where popstars, actors and the directors of independent film companies rub shoulders with bikers, sea dogs and the thousand odd county council staff who clutter up the pubs lunchtimes and weekends. The Mecca of these minor movie moguls is Stiwdio Barcud, the vast and lavish film studio built at the back of the town's rambling industrial estate.

The phenomenon that amazes visitors and is taken for granted by those who live there is that almost everybody speaks Welsh in this 'royal' town, and no matter how ugly you are, shop assistants will automatically greet you as *'Del'*, a casual term of endearment meaning handsome or pretty, or even *'Cyw'*, meaning 'chick' (regardless of your sex). The Welsh spoken by the native *Cofis* is however a guttural dialect consisting of obscure words and phrases that would put any protocol jargon to shame.

COLWYN BAY *(Bae Colwyn)*

Colwyn Bay is a comparatively new town between Old Colwyn *(Hen Golwyn)* and Rhos-on-Sea *(Llandrillo)* and basically is a three-mile stretch of promenade. Unkind observers have been known to state that most of the town's inhabitants are older than the buildings they live in. Nevertheless, it's a thriving holiday resort even in winter—when the weather's actually warmer, according to some. Bath-chairs, travel rugs and tartan thermos flasks are recommended if you want to blend in with your surroundings.

CONWY

Every Welsh trunk road with a '5' in its number has at least one notorious traffic bottle-neck. The A55 has Conwy—but only for the time being, it would seem. Work is under way on an ambitious project—under way being the appropriate expression. A tunnel under the river Conwy will bypass the town and put an end to mid-summer traffic jams in the town centre. Or so the planners hope. Conwy enjoys a reputation as one of North Wales' premier tourist attractions—mainly due to Edward I's castle, one of the country's finest. From the town's largest residence to the tiniest: on the quayside is the widely-publicised smallest house in Britain—stand in the kitchen and you can dust the bedroom ceiling with your head.

Bridge fanatics are also well catered for—not the North-South, shin-kicking variety, but the architectural version. Crossing the river near the castle are three of them—a tubular railway bridge by Robert Stephenson (the first in Britain to be built before being moved to its actual site), the soon-to-be-relieved road bridge and, in between, another example of Thomas Telford's expertise with suspension bridges.

DOLGELLAU

Another town which has become subject to a bypass operation. Narrow streets with numerous (absolutely necessary) one-way systems are the order of the day. Standing in the shadow of the imposing Cader Idris range, the town forms probably the easiest starting point for those hardy souls intent on climbing the mountain's 2,927 feet—via the Foxes' Path. When they get there, they should be advised against spending the night on the peak. An old myth persists that anyone who does that will wake up in the morning either a poet or a madman. Some would argue that they can't have been all there to go up in the first place.

For all those interested in ancient religious ruins (by this, we don't mean retired Presbyterian ministers), a mile or so from Dolgellau stands the remains of Cymer Abbey *(Abaty Cymer),* founded by the Cistercians in 1199. If your emotions are stirred by the mineral rather than the spiritual, grab a pan, roll up your trousers and try your luck in the myriad Mawddach valley streams. The area achieved fame for the numerous local gold mines (now closed). After all, Welsh gold has been used for the majority of the Windsor dynasty's wedding rings—although that hasn't been a good omen of late.

HOLYHEAD *(Caergybi)*

One of the Welsh escape routes to the Emerald Isle, best avoided during the days approaching rugby internationals between Wales and Ireland. The discerning visitor will find that Holyhead's attractions aren't very mountainous. Holyhead mountain towers to an incredible 719 feet—but the views more than make up for it. On a clear day, you'll glimpse Ireland, the Isle of Man (which disproves the much-vaunted theory that no man is an island), Snowdon and the Cumbrian peaks. Ornithologists (bird watchers to all but themselves) tend to ignore such sights, favouring a downward view—the cliffs around South Stack light-house teem with seabirds during the nesting season. Climbers, on the other hand, can be seen all the year round.

Due to its close proximity to the port of Dun

Laoghaire, Holyhead is, sadly for everybody except the local barons, a drugs heartland where heroin and hashish are the major import and export blackmarket trade.

LLANDUDNO

This seaside resort has everything for the discriminating visitor—a beach, beautiful walks, a fine pier, sports facilities, evening shows and splendid views of Snowdonia. The two headlands—the Great Orme and Little Orme—can be reached by cabin lift or tramway. From the top, on a clear day, you might be able to spot a local resident. Those unfortunate tourists not entirely at ease with the Welsh language who mistakenly book a two week holiday in Llandrindod, may often be spotted walking forlornly around the town looking for the pier.

It is said that Lewis Carroll was inspired by Llandudno to write *Alice in Wonderland*. 'Well,' I hear you say, 'I dudno that!'

The foregoing joke is perhaps typical of the Welsh sense of humour which, in the Welsh tongue, relies heavily upon the deliberate misuse of words. In the English tongue this is called 'Making a political speech'.

LLANFAIR PWLLGWYNGYLL GO-GER Y CHWYRNDROBWLL LLANTYSILIO GO-GO-GOCH

Certain cynical Welsh patriots have translated this very long place name as 'Birmingham-by-the-Sea'. This is by no means an accurate translation as it omits reference to many other parts of the Midlands. In fact, the name refers to the churches associated with two saints—Mair and Tysilio. This is the most quaint and most poetic Welsh place name dedicated to the memory of saints— of which there are about 500 commemorated in towns and villages all over Wales. But who, you might ask, was Saint Twit of 'Llantwit Major' *(Llanilltud Fawr)* fame? Was it Illtud, or did they canonise the local landowner?

Village children earn their pocket money during the holidays by reciting the name to busloads of doting American tourists with plenty of pennies to squander.

Because of the ever-increasing number of middle-class people who come to live here, the place has been nicknamed 'Volvograd', which is particularly apt as there is also a Volvo garage here!

A mile or so from the village is the Menai Strait, on whose banks dwells the famous artist Kyffin Williams and a statue of Nelson looking out to sea. Another landmark of the village is the Marquess Column, and it is possible to walk up the 117 steps.

LLANUWCHLLYN

If you wanted to be cruel, Llanuwchllyn could best be described as a one-horse-town where someone shot the horse. But if cruelty is not in your nature, this small village at the southern end of Bala Lake is one of the cradles of Welsh culture. As you turn into the village, you'll notice two statues—O. M. Edwards and Ifan ab Owen Edwards, father and son of this parish—whose contribution to the Welsh way of life is almost immeasurable. Between them they revolutionised education, founded Welsh children's magazines, and founded Urdd Gobaith Cymru (the Welsh League of Youth). Glanllyn, two miles away, is the site of one of the Urdd's two summer camps, where children from schools all over Wales come every summer. But if you're in search of steamy goings-on, look no further than across the lake from Glanllyn. The Bala Lake narrow gauge railway runs alongside Bala Lake—originality not being one of the area's strong points—from Bala to the village, while Meirionnydd's highest mountain—Aran Fawddwy—towers nearby. Only 50 feet higher than Cader Idris, locals would have you believe that it's only higher because they carried several hundred stones and rocks to the peak to attain superiority.

LLANYSTUMDWY

Visitors to this enchanted village will be drawn there by the spell of that great Welsh statesman David Lloyd George. Many called him 'the Welsh wizard', probably because he miraculously changed himself from a fervent Welsh nationalist into a royalist sycophant within a matter of a few years. This amazing metamorphosis set a trend for many later Welsh politicians who, once elected to Parliament, performed stunning sleights of hand. One of the most spectacular feats was performed by Jim (call me Lord) Callaghan who, when Prime Minister, managed to raise his right hand for devolution while at the same time waving two fingers behind his back. The reverse of this trick has recently been attempted without much success by Neil (call me Welsh) Kinnock.

LLŶN PENINSULA *(Pen Llŷn)*

Fervently nationalist, and one of the few remaining strongholds of the language, the influx of English immigrants threatens to drive the indigenous Welsh-speaking population into the sea. No doubt with this in mind, the settlers have kindly provided transport in some areas, notably the town of Aber-soch, with its yacht-filled harbour. In high summer, the only Welsh you'll find here is along the rim of a pound coin (the leek version). Other areas battle to retain their Welshness, while one village is actively promoting the language. Nant Gwrtheyrn, on the peninsula's north-west coast, houses the National Language Centre, where hundreds come every year to learn the Language of Heaven.

From Heaven on the northern side to Hell on the southern—Hell's Mouth *(Porth Neigwl)* is another of the area's notoriously dangerous coastal waters. Where this leaves Starcoast World (Butlin's with a name change), I'm not quite sure.

PORTHMADOG

Another case of the same old story. Another yacht-filled harbour for ocean-bound Welsh-speakers, this time complete with harbourside apartments and maisonettes (mostly English-owned) so that the mass emigration can be witnessed from the comfort of your own armchair. Back in the twelfth century, if you believe the legend, the harbour witnessed another emigrant—Madog—whose thirteen ships left the shores of Wales *en route* to discover America. So many countries claim that one of their men discovered it—but if it was discovered today, they might all vehemently deny having done so. Some theorise that Madog actually landed in Ireland because it was in the way.

Those of you who approach along the main road from the east, prepare to dig deep into your pockets—there's a toll to pay. Forget the American Express Gold Card, however—5p should be within your reach. If 5p seems a trifle steep, there is an alternative route, tortuous and twisting, to Tremadog—famous as the birthplace of Lawrence of Arabia and not much else.

PORTMEIRION

Gwynedd's premier tourist attraction is a little corner of Italy in Snowdonia. Architect Clough Williams-Ellis had a dream of creating an Italianate village resembling the pretty harbours of Portofino or Sorrento—Portmeirion is the result. Some would consider it more of a nightmare than a dream. Countless films have been shot here, but the best-known is the cult television series *The Prisoner*. Every year, a horde of bizarre folk spend a week in the village recreating scenes from the programme. Check in case your visit clashes—these people are in desperate need of psychiatric counselling.

PWLLHELI

The capital of the Llŷn Peninsula, where farmers go to market on Wednesdays and round the pubs raising hell on Saturday nights. A quiet enough place in winter when the sand-blown promenade is deserted, it undergoes a complete transformation in summer when holidaymakers from the Butlins camp just outside town are let loose on the streets. Burgers, bangers, chips, chips, chips, Party Time, stand-up comedians, glamorous grannies, fruit machines, pool tables—special cultural holidays are enjoyed here by visitors from Liverpool and Birmingham—burgers, bangers, beer, chips, chips, chips . . . The early members of Plaid Cymru (the national political party of Wales founded in Pwllheli) are probably doing triple backward somersaults in their graves when they hear the 'ritual murder of vowels' (according to the famous Anglo-Welsh poet R.S.Thomas who lives nearby in the tiny village of Rhiw) of the Brummie dialect. The headquarters of Dwyfor County Council are based in Pwllheli in ugly 1960s buildings near the harbour, which is in the process of being renovated, to the delight of filthy-rich non-Welsh-speaking yacht-owners.

SNOWDON *(Yr Wyddfa)*

For the even more ambitious, the legendary peaks of Snowdonia challenge the most hardy tourists. You can climb up, walk up the gentle slopes or take the mountain railway, always remembering not to get off while the train is still in motion (this is a local bye-law).

TAL-Y-LLYN

One of the most photographed spots in the whole of Wales—try buying a calendar filled with Welsh views

Trawsfynydd nuclear power station.

where Tal-y-llyn doesn't feature. The lake is now owned by the Welsh Water Authority, presumably as back-up should one of the reservoirs supplying Merseyside and the Midlands dry up. Unlike the Bala Lake railway, the Tal-y-llyn railway is nowhere near the lake, but two miles away in the village of Abergynolwyn. Full marks for originality—confusing tourists is high on the list of popular local hobbies.

TRAWSFYNYDD

For something a little bit different try Trawsfynydd. Here is the first inland nuclear power station in Britain. (Who said England got all the best things!) At night Trawsfynydd has its own special aurora borealis as the mountain sheep glow in truly Jacob-like coats of many colours. Two centre holidays can be arranged—since Trawsfynydd is now twinned with Chernobyl.

TRYWERYN

Here's a spot for all water-sports enthusiasts. A man-made lake created to supply water to a major English city can now offer a host of activities to the get-up-and-go tourist. But watch out all you water-skiers! If the water level drops you might just have a nasty surprise as your skis hit the top of the chapel that was drowned along with the rest of this Welsh village.

DE MORGANNWG (South Glamorgan)

BARRY *(Y Barri)*

The rural peace of Barry was shattered in the 1840s when work started on building the town's first dock—a tribute to the importance of the coal-mining valleys of the Rhondda.

As a treat for children of all ages, there are many fine beaches all around the coast of Wales. Barry Island offers something for all the family—a fine sandy beach a few shades lighter than the sea that brings in exciting flotsam and jetsam—sea-shells, sewage and, more tragically, the occasional body of an unhappy inmate of the nearby holiday camp, dashed on the rocks while trying to escape. The fun fair is well laid out and carefully planned. After you've paid half a week's wages for two hot dogs, a stick of candy floss and a carton of whelks you can spend the other half on the roller-coaster and big wheel, and having emptied your stomach and your wallet, you can use your Barclaycard for a round of jumbo sausages and chips and so on until you get a rare experience of perpetual motions.

For all parents among you, there will come a time when your children will suddenly start asking embarrassing questions like 'Mum, where do bananas come from?' Now you'll be able to tell them that a lot come from Barry, or at least that's where they reach these shores.

CARDIFF *(Caerdydd)*

The capital city of Wales, where you are more likely to hear Urdu spoken than Welsh. Cardiff, the city of contrasting sounds; the wailing and gnashing of teeth coming from the National Stadium as the Welsh rugby team lose their match against Greenland; the busking of mendicant musicians in Burger Boulevard (formerly Queen Street); the gargling of sherry down dossers' throats; the clinking of credit cards in the Holiday Inn.

Cardiff—like Swansea and Newport—is having its docks transformed by planners and estate agents. Incoming yuppies can buy a house described as 'executive' (over-priced), 'linked' (terraced), in the 'marina' (near a bit of polluted water with a few boats on it).

Cardiff is fast becoming a cosmopolitan city reflected in the variety of national costumes worn by its inhabitants. In some parts of the city yashmaks and saris grace the scene while in the lounge bar of a local pub an indigenous Cardiffian sports his newest vest annd tattoos.

Cardiff castle is a major tourist attraction. Its ornate interior decoration—like its smaller version at Castell Coch, designed by the same architect—cunningly combines ostentation with sumptous vulgarity—rather like the Mediaeval banquet held nightly.

But where better to appreciate the history and culture of Wales than in the National Museum at Cardiff. Not that the museum is exclusively filled with Welsh exhibits. The Art Gallery is noted for its fine collection of world-renowned artists, not least for its old masters who still provoke animated debate among experts. Are they really from the brush of Rubens? Or were they part of a collection of masterpieces given away free in a breakfast cereal promotion campaign? Why not go and see them and make up your own mind?

Perhaps the most famous piece of sculpture in the museum is 'The Kiss' by Rodin, the pen (or chisel) name of Rod(dy) Llewell(yn), a bright young Welsh artist who is reported to have used actual living models to construct his massive work. Many connoisseurs and cognoscenti, however, agree that the female figure was probably based on an early lithograph of Queen Victoria and the male figure is based on an even earlier photograph of Queen Victoria.

COWBRIDGE *(Y Bont-faen)*

In London, those with more money than sense (aristocracy, Sloane Rangers, Hooray Henrys, diplomats etc) make a bee-line for Knightsbridge and the top people's store, Harrod's. Even those who don't use fivers to light fires visit sometimes—to buy tangerines or suchlike—just for the kudos of carrying the famous green carrier bag. The Cardiff equivalent is Cowbridge. Anything bought in this town, which is about twelve miles west of the capital, reeks of the exclusive. Anybody who shops here is making a kind of statement about their wealth—rather like the man who drives a Bentley. Of course, he could afford to buy a Rolls-Royce, but he doesn't derive great pleasure from flashing his wealth about the place.

LLANDAFF *(Llandaf)*

Even nearer to the centre of Cardiff is a quiet spot graced by a beautiful cathedral. Llandaff is a select suburb of the capital city with its public schools, its theological college and rowing club. The village, of course, has the obligatory Chinese Take-Away and Tandoori restaurant but fights on a Saurday night must be conducted according to the Queensbury Rules.

The BBC has its Wales headquarters here. Rather like the Vatican, this is a city within a city with its own

language ('Hello Darling/*Cariad*'—and that's just the commissionaire!), its own culture (drinking on the job is not permitted unless it's part of the script or written into the employee's contract) and its own sense of destiny which is emblazoned in its coat-of-arms, a rough translation from the Latin being: 'We are here to entertain, educate and generally look down on all those berks who are daft enough to pay the licence fee'.

Credentials for entry into the higher echelons of this august company include an undistinguished degree, the ability to speak Welsh and a totally unfounded sense of one's own importance. Visitors to the BBC are welcome but may be frisked before admission. This is not because of any security risk; the commissionaire (see above) just enjoys doing it.

PENARTH

Penarth, literally translated as bear's head, is a curious mixture of bistros and blue rinse brigades. If you're looking for something more exciting and vibrant than a walk to the end of the pier, this is not the place for you. The flowers on the promenade are pretty, but most people seek something more when their holidays come around. On most beaches, it takes topless sunbathing to cause an uproar. For staid and sedate Penarth, the very sight of a naked female ankle keeps the local paper's letters column busy for weeks.

THE VALE OF GLAMORGAN *(Bro Morgannwg)*

These acres of idyllic villages and pasture were once the centre of Welsh culture. It was here that the Welsh language flourished in verse and praise. Today its network of small settlements betray the area's later secession to alien influences. The very names—Peterston, Bonvilston, St. George's, St. Nicholas—could be the names of villages in Surrey. To live in the Vale is to have 'arrived'. How comforting to know that most Welsh people don't even want to start the journey.

Penarth pier.

GORLLEWIN MORGANNWG (West Glamorgan)

CRAIG-Y-NOS

This small village at the head of the Swansea Valley owes its fame to something completely different from the coal-mining heritage of the rest of the area. It was to Craig-y-nos castle that famed operatic prima donna Adelina Patti fled for refuge far from the bright lights of success—and you can't get much further than this. She bought it in 1871 and spent part of her lavish fortune on improving it, including her own private theatre.

But after her death in 1919, it was gifted to the Welsh National Memorial Association and converted into a hospital—giving the 'theatre' a whole new purpose.

A mile or so further north is another attraction which draws tourists from far and wide—the Dan-yr-Ogof Caves, a complex system of underground caverns and grottoes formed in the local limestone rocks. Some sceptics have suggested that the retention of the Welsh name—for which South Wales is not particularly noted—is because the translation ('Under the Cave Caves') would sound funny.

GOWER PENINSULA (Penrhyn Gŵyr)

As most tourist guides would have you believe, the Gower Peninsula is one of the last unspoilt areas of outstanding natural beauty in Wales. Unspoilt in this context means that the area is connected to the natural grid: there are caravan parks and countless shops selling dragon souvenirs and scenic postcards, but despite all this, the views are still wonderful. Like Snowdonia after driving through Bethesda, Gower's appeal is strengthened by having just passed through Swansea.

Attractions which don't depend on the breathtaking views are few, but it is worth mentioning the famous Paviland caves, where a human headless skeleton was unearthed in 1823. The bones, stained in red ochre, were known as the Red Lady of Paviland until later excavations proved that the lady was in fact a man who lived during the Old Stone Age. If all they had to work on was bones, how this was proved is a bit of a mystery . . .

MUMBLES (Y Mwmbls)

How this area to the south-west of Swansea was named also remains a bit of a mystery. Local drinkers who have attempted the famed 'Mumbles Mile'—buying (and drinking) a wee snort at all the watering holes situated along the rambling promenade—put forward the theory that it's because everyone who has successfully negotiated the jaunt end up mumbling. Their argument falls apart when confronted with the fact that the name was there before the hotels.

NEATH *(Castell-nedd)*

A small West Wales town, proud of its nearly invincible rugby team. This small town has Roman and mediaeval remains and, on the rugby field, somewhat Neanderthal connections. Nearby is the impressive Pensgynor Wildlife Park with its great variety of birds, seals and other animals. The children who used to enjoy a romp with the Park's chimpanzees must now remain safely segregated since the baby chimps have been known to catch nasty diseases from their human playmates.

PONT ABRAM

Strictly speaking, this isn't a proper place at all. Pont Abram is the services point at the westernmost end of the M4 motorway and the natural habitat of police panda car drivers getting into the right frame of mind by paying through the nose for brown water which is classed as tea and hungry-looking families sharing a bread roll between them as they moan about leaving the Am-Ex Gold Card at home.

PONTARDDULAIS

This town on the river Loughor *(Llwchwr)* west of Swansea owes its growth to the 1870s tinplate works and its fame to a musical tradition underlined by the local male voice choir. The town is now skirted by the M4, and a few years ago thirsty Carmarthenshire residents flocked across the river for a Sunday drink. Now the entire south is 'wet' so you don't have to go there if you don't want to.

PORT TALBOT

A beautiful seaside resort on the South Wales coast. Beautiful compared to Widness, that is. When driving west on the M4 with your mother-in-law sitting in the back, think twice before complaining about her total lack of control in the bowel department—you could be driving past Port Talbot.

SWANSEA *(Abertawe)*

Its association with the world-renowned poet Dylan Thomas—he drank there, as well as there and everywhere—has attracted many tourists. Scholars have suggested that the setting for *Under Milk Wood,* Llareggub (Buggerall backwards, if you'll excuse the expression) is a fairly accurate description of Swansea's list of attractions.

You may enjoy the leisure centre at Swansea and the fine new offices of the West Glamorgan County Council. Swansea is truly a city of miracles. Not only has it arisen out of the ashes of the World War II blitz, but it has managed to find enough ratepayers' money to build monuments to its august elected members despite an all-Wales record of homelessness.

Finding an empty home isn't a problem, especially if you wander down to the exotically-named Maritime Quarter (was it thus named because a quarter of the flats there are empty? Or because they're now worth a quarter of the price paid for them?). The forgiving nature of the Welsh is also very much in evidence here, with names such as Mannheim Quay ('Come in Mr Schwarzkopf. Never mind about razing the city to dust. Have a cup of tea.').

Shopping in Swansea is quite and experience. The city centre is dominated by a huge complex called the Quadrant Centre, where you can walk for miles without seeing a hint of sky. During the Christmas rush, you can walk for miles without seeing a hint of the floor.

Those who drive rusty K-reg Beetles will find a spiritual home in Swansea, as these are the only vehicles which are always left untouched by four foot tall joyriders. Even Robin Reliants aren't safe; apparently they take the body shells off and use the chassis as skateboards.

At weekends the nightclubs are swarming with bimbos wearing warpaint and little else and tattooed thugs looking for a woman to drag home by the hair or better still, a fight. This savage tribe is called the Swansea Jacks.

Night out in Swansea.

MORGANNWG GANOL (Mid Glamorgan)

The valley towns of Merthyr, Aberdare, Port Talbot and Ebbw Vale summon up a bygone era of coal and steel. Now, thanks to experts, a typical coal tip has been removed by numbering each lump of coal and reconstructing the huge mound at St Fagan's Folk Museum.

The Big Pit near Blaenafon in Gwent also offers the tourist an opportunity to imagine life below ground. Once you have seen Blaenafon, you might wonder why the miners bothered to come up.

Enterprising schemes have now been put in motion to restore the valleys to their former green glory. The accent is now on recreation and tourism. For an off-beat experience try the half-finished ski-slope near Merthyr or the deserted Wild West town in the Rhondda. The Garden Festival near Ebbw Vale promises to be the world's shortest tourist event as the local sheep do not require tickets for admission.

ABERDARE (Aberdâr)

Iron and coal were the catalysts for Aberdare's initial

expansion, although the town itself is one of the oldest settlements in the South Wales valleys. Situated in the upper reaches of the Cynon valley, the industrial decline which has struck the entire area is very much in evidence in Aberdare as well. Ann Clwyd, the local Member of Parliament, could loudly proclaim that she is the prettiest MP in Wales. And should any other Welsh MP express doubts about her statement, she could alter it to 'the prettiest female MP'. Not difficult, as she's the only one.

BRIDGEND *(Pen-y-bont ar Ogwr)*

On the western fringe of the scenic Vale of Glamorgan, Bridgend seems to have been dropped in to rural countryside. It suffered less than most during the thirties depression, mainly because the local industrial scene wasn't as coal-orientated as other towns. Careful drivers abound here—the presence of the South Wales Police training school makes the M4 around Bridgend one of the few stretches of motorway in Britain where anybody actually takes much notice of the legal speed limit.

CAERPHILLY *(Caerffili)*

It's difficult to know how to describe Caerphilly—is it the town with the largest castle in Wales that had a cheese named after it, or is it the town that had a cheese named after it with the largest castle in Wales? Leaving historians and gourmets to argue the toss, there really is little else to see.

It is a modest town dominated by its castle—the second largest in Britain. Its unique feature is its leaning tower which lists at a greater degree than the tower of Pisa. Recent research has proved, however, that the castle tower is perfectly perpendicular and the whole of Caerphilly is subsiding at an acute angle and sliding inexorably into the moat. Underwater shopping at the town's Co-op could well be a major tourist attraction in years to come.

LLANTRISANT

This village still retains an olde worlde atmosphere even though it is only eight miles from Cardiff. Llantrisant was the home of the Victorian eccentric Dr William Price. He considered himself to be a descendant of the Druids and he went from village to village dressed in a flowing cloak. At the age of 83 he cremated his young son and was consequently taken to court where he was acquitted of all charges.

Llantrisant was granted a charter in 1346 and still has a court 'leet' and a body of freemen who meet for a dinner every year in order to try to find out what a court 'leet' is. Today, Llantrisant is the home of the Royal Mint. This is popular with people of the adjacent South Wales valleys still suffering from unemployment. They are allowed in free of charge to come and see whan a ten pound note looks like.

MAESTEG

If this town was known by its literal translation of 'fair field', every visitor would justifiably seek compensation under the Trades Descriptions Act. Like many towns in the area, it grew (and shrivelled) in tandem with the coal industry. Many of the town's chapels, which once sprouted like mushrooms, no longer echo to the sound of hymn-singing (if you want to hear this, try the local pub)—doors have been closed, pews have been ripped out and organs transplanted to be replaced by boys' clubs and carpet warehouses.

MERTHYR TUDFUL

Merthyr's growth to its present size began in earnest at the onset of the Industrial Revolution, when large iron-works were established at Dowlais, Cyfarthfa and Penydarren to exploit the area's varied mineral wealth. But the name belongs to another age—legend has it that a British princess, Tudful, was martyred for her Christian faith. Unkind souls now theorise that martyrdom is synonymous with stopping in the town. Since the thirties' depression, when heavy industry moved to more con-venient coastal locations, decimated Merthyr's economy and left a legacy of massively high unemployment, the town has struggled to return to some kind of normality—and these days is more likely to be associated with Hoover washing machines than a place where industrial prosperity once created a 'boom town'.

MOUNTAIN ASH (Aberpennar)

Most major towns in Mid Glamorgan look back to the thirties as a turning point in their histories—Mountain Ash is no exception. Indeed, it suffered more than most, with a 20% decrease in population, as workers who flooded in to find work flooded out again when none was forthcoming.

PONTYPRIDD

It's a sad fact that when talking about Pontypridd, most people don't associate it with the area's industrial heydey; they don't even link it with the old single-span bridge over the river Taff which gave the town its name. No, Pontypridd is the birthplace of Tom Jones—a man who apparently stuck a miner's helmet down the front of his trousers, wiggled his hips and embarked on a singing career, belting out such timeless classics as 'The Green Green Grass of Home'. Curiously enough, it's easier to find yellow, yellow sand in Pontypridd than green,

green grass.

PORTH-CAWL

This resort—the closest thing to a Welsh equivalent of Blackpool—gained popularity when thousands of miners from the surrounding valleys thronged there to wash those little parts a tin bath in front of the fire just couldn't reach. Nowadays, the area has been invaded by the various gruesomely-shaped metal objects known as rides which come together to form what constitutes a pleasure park—chills, thrills and stomach-churning spills that induce candy-floss-and-ice-cream-laden vomit.

RHONDDA VALLEYS (Y Rhondda)

The two valleys of the Rhondda Fawr and the Rhondda Fach were the very heart of the South Wales Coalfield and the number of towns bear testimony to the thousands who moved into the area in search of employment—Treherbert, Treorci, Tonypandy, Porth, Tylorstown, Ferndale and Maerdy, to name but a few. The last pit in the Rhondda was at Maerdy, now closed after the area was ravaged by the desolation of the year-long miners' strike in the mid-eighties. This desolation is obvious by the surroundings, although some waste heaps have been re-seeded in an attempt to blot out the area's industrial decay. But the people themselves seem oblivious to it—a breed apart, fiercely proud and possessing an iron will for life, despite the difficulties. A strange irony is that most of the towns boast one institution which is as out of place as an igloo in the Sahara—the Conservative Club. Politics are seemingly set aside as they become just another place to have a drink, and even more flock through their doors when an election looms—a pint tastes even better when it's bought by the forever-doomed Tory candidate.

POWYS

Winding roads, beautiful scenery and hardly any people—paradise! Powys has been the seat of two self-governing nations. In 1404 Owain Glyndŵr set up his Parliament in Machynlleth and more recently a second-hand bookseller declared VDI for Hay-on-Wye. The beauty of Powys is that if tomorrow the whole county became self-governing, hardly anyone would notice.

BRECON *(Aberhonddu)*

That strangely peculiar creature the jazz-fiend will no doubt have heard of, as well as visited Brecon during the annual jazz festival held there every summer. But if trad has the same effect on you as bucket of damp lard, don't despair—it's quite normal for the rest of the year. George Melly does have a house there though—so it might be prudent to steer clear anyway, unless you actually like fat men in loud suits. The town boasts the lavish headquarters of Welsh Water, a cathedral, the Christ's College public school which maintains a keen rivalry on the rugby field with its counterpart at Llandovery, and a picturesque golf course. Who could ask for anything more? . . . One at a time, please.

BRECON BEACONS *(Bannau Brycheiniog)*

Hands up everyone who thinks that the Brecon Beacons are a local American-football team. In actual fact, they are mountains which form the centre of one of the three Welsh National Parks and are the highest mountains in South Wales. Though they reach nearly 3,000 feet in places, they are nowhere near as spectacular as the Snowdonia peaks—but are still as dangerous in the regular swirling mists.

CLYWEDOG RESERVOIR *(Llyn Clywedog)*

High in the mountains west of Llanidloes, along the mountain road to Machynlleth, lies the reservoir at Clywedog. Many deep and inaccessible valleys were drowned in the 1960s to form the lake, which is very impressive when viewed from the numerous parking places high above its shores. The usual road improvements which go hand in hand with such developments were carried out, but once you pass the boundary of land bought by Birmingham Corporation, it reverts to its previous existence as a tortuous and narrow beast. And check your brakes before you set out. Nothing depresses the sightseeing tourist more than stopping in a lay-by to take in the view and uttering the words 'That car's just the same as mine' as a familiar family saloon plummets into the deep blue below. You have been warned.

CRICKHOWELL *(Crucywel)*

Keen bird-watchers should avoid this Usk valley town like the plague. There might be some feathered friends about, but they are constantly being given coronaries by a more recent migrant species—hang-gliders. Although lower in intellect than their natural flying counterparts, they have taken over the surrounding skies and as well as making the best use of rising thermals, they appear to have an added incentive to soar for longer. If they landed in the town itself, they would soon be struck down by a terminal case of boredom.

Crickhowell has also gained some fame (or should that read notoriety) through Nicholas Edwards, former Tory Secretary of State for Wales, who adopted the name of the town for his elevation to the House of Lords. As his constituency was in far-off Pembrokeshire, this is rather curious, until one realises that most of that institution's residents also spend much of their year in blissful hibernation.

ELAN VALLEY *(Cwm Elan)*

This area of mid-Wales has more dams than a successful stud farm, all supplying water to the jewel that is Birmingham. The reservoirs of Caban Coch, Garreg Ddu, Craig Goch and Claerwen all still look distinctly out of place amid the surrounding empty moorlands, despite having been there for most of this century. But anyone who could stand with his hand on his heart and state that they aren't an improvement must either have a pathological fear of water or an unnatural sympathy to the plight of the sheep. And even the sheep might express a tiny preference for watching the odd dinghy sailing by as opposed to chewing reeds all day. Not that anyone's ever put their feelings to the vote . . .

EPPYNT MOUNTAIN *(Mynydd Epynt)*

While the sheep on Eppynt mountain might decide that a quiet session of reed-chewing would be infinitely preferable to what they are lumbered with, they daren't even dream of spying a passing white sail. Eppynt—in the triangle between Brecon, Builth Wells and Llandovery—has been taken over by the British Army as a vast training ground, although in what way military manœuvres against a regiment of sheep can possibly be of any use in an actual battle situation is extremely doubtful . . . apart from the Falklands conflict. Low-flying exercises have rendered the woolly creatures a trifle blasé to the oncoming roar of a sound-barrier-shattering Jaguar—which is why the RAF feel obliged to bombard the rest of the country's sheep to test the animals' reactions. Very handy should some bored wing-commander declare war on New Zealand . . .

LLANDRINDOD WELLS *(Llandrindod)*

Further north, away from the hustle and bustle of discos, bingos and fat white ladies oozing out of black bathing costumes, lies the tranquil town of Llandrindod Wells. This is still a working spa but it is also a place of mystery.

The ten yearly census confirms that there are people still actually living there but to the inexperienced eye it is the veritable Marie Celeste of Wales. Perhaps you will glimpse the furtive fluttering of lace curtains in the window of an erstwhile fashionable dwelling or perhaps hear the distant drone of guests snoring as they sit in the comfortable lounge of a temperance hotel. Llandrindod is definitely the ideal place to go for those tourists for whom the epitome of excitement is queuing for Max Bygraves' autograph.

LLANELWEDD

Venue for the Royal Welsh Agricultural Show. If you believe that one sheep—or for that matter one hamster—looks, or smells, like any other one then you are mistaken. A veritable cornucopia of cows, bonanza of bullocks and plethora of pigs will pass before you in a coruscating cavalcade where Beauty and the Beast become as one! Now, the Animal Welfare and Vegetarian groups have combined to organize a Fringe Festival.

LLANFYLLIN

Not many have found any reason to stop in this quiet town—most visitors pass through on their way to or from two water-orientated tourist attractions: one natural, one man-made. The latter, Lake Vyrnwy, covers another village drowned by the Liverpool Corporation to quench that city's thirst. The name of that village, Llanwddyn, lives on in a new settlement just below the dam—presumably safe in the knowledge that, so far, no village has been drowned by the same reservoir twice. Further north is the natural attraction of Pistyll Rhaeadr, a spectacular waterfall which was once listed as one of the Seven Wonders of Wales. In the nearby village of Llanrhaeadr-ym-Mochnant in 1588, Bishop William Morgan translated the Bible into Welsh—a feat which passed largely unnoticed over the border, where Francis Drake was busy playing bowls and repelling the Spanish Armada.

LLANGURIG

Avid students of Welsh road-signs might gain the impression that all roads in Wales lead to Llangurig. So when they eventually get there, they expect a sprawling metropolis teeming with business suits and high-powered conglomerates. Nothing, as they say, could be further from the truth. True, it has a church and two pubs and a scattering of houses, but what really sets the place apart are the roads. The town stands near the junction of the main north-south trunk road with the main mid-Wales east-west route. The laws of probability are ideally demonstrated here i.e. if you are approaching the town from any given direction by car, driving behind a hulking sixteen-wheel articulated lorry, the lorry will always go where you're headed.

LLANIDLOES

A sleepy market town five miles north of Llangurig (which is positively comatose in comparison), Llanidloes woke up in 1839 for a short but well-documented Chartist rebellion, before hitting the snooze button to rest some more. Although not many of the residents will have noticed, Llanidloes is now served by a bypass. And not before time. The town's main square is the location of an early seventeenth-century market hall and bears testimony to the often-laid charge that road designers live on another planet. The market hall is slap-bang in the middle of a crossroads—with all exits so narrow that the only confident road-users in Llanidloes are cyclists. Some would argue that the road designers were working hand in glove with local businessmen—one wide load would block up traffic for a good few hours, so that frustrated steering-wheel-chewing motorists would eventually give up the ghost and do a bit of shopping.

MACHYNLLETH

Here in the Dyfi Valley is the picturesque setting for Owain Glyndŵr's Welsh Parliament and the more enduring empire of Laura Ashley. Although this megastore has now relocated its headquarters, its influence lingers on in the parlours and bedrooms of the bourgeoisie. There was much discussion that the capital of Wales should have been Machynlleth instead of Cardiff. Since very few members of the Government of that time knew where Wales was, let alone Machynlleth, Cardiff had a head start since most people had heard of Tiger Bay and Shirley Bassey.

Just a couple of miles north of Machynlleth is the Centre for Alternative Technology *(Canolfan y Dechnoleg Amgen)*. This was developed some years ago when Wales was becoming 'green' while the rest of Britain was still 'blue' and occasionally 'red'. Here you can see energy being generated in various novel ways. Ten male voice choirs singing in rota throughout twenty-four hours direct their voices to a large wheel which is then turned over cogs. This in turn propels another wheel in the same building—a converted electricity sub-station— which activates a robot constructed entirely out of recycled gas cookers. The robot advances holding a crude stick in either hand down a ramp towards a redundant coalmerchant who—on receipt of the two sticks— rubs them vigourously together thus creating a spark which is directed towards a candle made of organically produced beeswax. The candle is then ignited.

This entirely 'green' and alternative operation lasts for the duration of one rendition of 'Men of Harlech' which—discounting encores and breaks for beer— amounts to twenty-three mintues. In one day, therefore, a total of sixty-two and a half candles are set alight. In terms of power, this would be sufficient to heat five microwave suppers for two or to defrost three members of Merched y Wawr (see text).

Windmills, watermills and solar panels are also to be seen at the Centre as well as innovative methods of insulating houses such as constructing them entirely out of polystyrene disposable beakers or filling the lofts with all-purpose chicken manure. This stops heat from escaping through the roof while at the same time ensuring a good crop of home grown mushrooms. The manure can also be used to power alternative vehicle engines, encourage hair growth (so far, in tests, only in relatively bald hamsters) and as a particularly piquant relish in veggieburgers.

Visitors to the Centre for Alternative Technology may wish to visit the site shop where souvenirs are on sale. Edible sandals and biodegradeable miners' lamps are just two of the selections of reasonably priced articles for sale. The next time you return to Wales you might see rows of terraced houses with glass roofs and special satellite dishes that can be used as woks. Wales will become the greenest of all green and pleasant lands.

NEWTOWN *(Y Drenewydd)*

This is the town where Robert Owen lived—the man whose vision of a socialist Utopia bore fruit in factory reform and the creation of the Co-operative Movement. Now along with the rest of any real socialist dreams, he lies buried in a derelict graveyard. The town lives on, just like politics in Wales—formless, unlovely and in urgent need of an inspirational architect.

OFFA'S DYKE *(Clawdd Offa)*

Stretching virtually the whole length of Wales, this fortification was constructed 1200 years ago by the King of Mercia, today's English Midlands, to keep out the marauding Welsh. The dyke proved largely ineffective, so they built Birmingham.

RHAYADER *(Rhaeadr Gwy)*

Pick a road, any road. In a sense, Rhayader is close to everywhere. In another, it's close to nowhere. Roads lead to Leominster, Builth Wells, the Elan Valley reservoirs and the disappointingly empty metropolis that is Llangurig. Take one of them.

SENNY BRIDGE *(Pontsenni)*

Near Brecon is a modern military encampment still undeveloped as a tourist attraction although it has been known to take the overflow of inmates at the camps at Barry Island and Pwllheli. Rumour has it that the discipline is slightly less strict at the Senny Bridge camp.

WELSHPOOL *(Y Trallwng)*

After Newtown, Welshpool is the least imaginatively named place in the old Montgomeryshire *(Sir Drefaldwyn)*, which was swallowed into the vast county of Powys during the local government reorganisation of 1974. A bustling market town—which is nowadays only bustling on market day—to which many flock for the excitement and the fast-paced lifestyle—mostly from Llanidloes and Llangurig.

If well-kept gardens set your heart a-flutter (is anyone who can be this bored still breathing?), then a visit to the nearby Powis Castle is a must. They were renovated by the landscape gardner Capability Brown early last century. If your heart is still beating to its usual rhythm, the nearest beach is at Barmouth . . .

Language books,
cookbooks,
songbooks,
art books,
political books...

...guide books,
storybooks,
childrens' books
—and more
in our free,
80 page
Catalogue!

Talybont
Ceredigion
Cymru SY24 5HE
tel. (0970) 832 304
fax. 832 782